GLOBAL REPERTOIRES

Global Repertoires

Popular music within and beyond the transnational
music industry

Edited by

ANDREAS GEBESMAIR
*Mediacult, International Research Institute for Media,
Communication and Cultural Development, Austria*

ALFRED SMUDITS
*Institute of Music Sociology, University of Music and
Performing Arts, Austria*

Aldershot • Burlington USA • Singapore • Sydney

Published by
Ashgate Publishing Ltd
Gower House
Croft Road
Aldershot
Hants GU11 3HR
England

Ashgate Publishing Company
131 Main Street
Burlington, VT 05401-5600 USA

Ashgate website: http://www.ashgate.com

British Library Cataloguing in Publication Data
Global repertoires : popular music within and beyond the
    transnational music industry. - (Ashgate popular and folk
    music series)
    1. Popular music 2. Globalization
    I. Gebesmair, Andreas II. Smudits, A.
    781.6'3

Library of Congress Cataloging-in-Publication Data
Global repertoires : popular music within and beyond the transnational music industry /
edited by Andreas Gebesmair, International Research Institute for Media,
Communication, and Cultural Development, Austria and Alfred Smudits, Institute of
Music Sociology, Austria.
        p.cm. -- (Ashgate popular and folk music series)
    Contains materials presented at a conference on music and globalization organized by
the International Research Institute for Media, Communication and Cultural
Development (Mediacult) and held Nov. 4-6, 1999 in Vienna, Austria.
    Includes bibliographical references.
    ISBN 0-7546-0526-4 (alk.paper)
    1. Popular music--History and criticism--Congresses. 2. Music trade--Congresses. 3.
Globalization--Congresses. I. Gebesmair, Andreas. II. Smudits, A. III. MEDIACULT.
IV. Series.

ML3470 .G56 2001
306.4'84   2001022817

ISBN 0 7546 0526 4

Printed and bound by Athenaeum Press, Ltd., Gateshead, Tyne & Wear.

Contents

List of Contributors

Alenka Barber-Kersovan, Germany
Executive Secretary of the Arbeitskreis Studium Populärer Musik, Hamburg

Susanne Binas, Germany
Research Assistant and lecturer at the Forschungszentrum populäre Musik, Humboldt-Universität zu Berlin

Joana Breidenbach, Germany
Anthropologist – journalist living in Berlin

Robert Burnett, Sweden
Professor of Media and Communication Studies at University of Karlstad

Gust de Meyer, Belgium
Associate Professor at the Department of Communication of the Catholic University of Leuven

Andreas Gebesmair, Austria
Research Assistant at Mediacult, International Research Institute, Vienna

Harald Huber, Austria
Assistant and lecturer of popular music at the University of Music and the Performing Arts, Vienna

Krister Malm, Sweden
General Director of the Swedish National Collections of Music, Stockholm

Keith Negus, UK
Senior Lecturer at the Department of Media and Communications, Goldsmiths College, University of London

Deborah Pacini Hernandez, USA
Associate Professor of American Civilization and Urban Studies at Brown University

Richard A. Peterson, USA
Professor of Sociology at Vanderbilt University

Keith Roe, Belgium
Director of the Media and Audience Research section of the Department of Communication Sciences of the Catholic University of Leuven

Alfred Smudits, Austria
Professor at the Institute of Music Sociology at the University of Music and Performing Arts, Vienna

Ina Zukrigl, Germany
Social anthropologist living in Berlin

General Editor's Series Preface

The upheaval that occurred in musicology during the last two decades of the twentieth century has created a new urgency for the study of popular music alongside the development of new critical and theoretical models. A relativistic outlook has replaced the universal perspective of modernism (the international ambitions of the 12-note style); the grand narrative of the evolution and dissolution of tonality has been challenged, and emphasis has shifted to cultural context, reception and subject position. Together, these have conspired to eat away at the status of canonical composers and categories of high and low in music. A need has arisen, also, to recognize and address the emergence of crossovers, mixed and new genres, to engage in debates concerning the vexed problem of what constitutes authenticity in music and to offer a critique of musical practice as the product of free, individual expression.

Popular musicology is now a vital and exciting area of scholarship, and the Ashgate Popular and Folk Music Series aims to present the best research in the field. Authors will be concerned with locating musical practices, values and meanings in cultural context, and may draw upon methodologies and theories developed in cultural studies, semiotics, poststructuralism, psychology and sociology. The series will focus on popular musics of the twentieth and twenty-first centuries. It is designed to embrace the world's popular musics from Acid Jazz to Zydeco, whether high tech or low tech, commercial or non-commercial, contemporary or traditional.

Professor Derek B. Scott
Chair of Music
University of Salford

Visit Project Pop: http://www.salford.ac.uk/FDTLpop/welcome.htm

Preface

This is an important and timely publication in the *Ashgate Popular and Folk Music Series*. For many people, globalization means, in cultural terms, an American entertainment empire that places the many and varied cultures of the world at the mercy of transnational corporations and their marketing teams. Some people see globalization as the spread of a consumer democracy. Andy Warhol once commented that no amount of wealth or power could buy you a better Coca-Cola than the one the next person was drinking. Compare that with the social elitism associated with France's best-known drink, Champagne. Yet, should we not be concerned, as are the writers here, that local and regional music cultures face an unprecedented onslaught from transnational industries and their ever-increasing production of cultural goods for global distribution? And what about the popular musicians who are promoted by these industries? Does the music business now have them in a stranglehold? Are they no more than cogs in a corporate machine?

In this book an international group of scholars are not seeking to provide easy answers to such complex questions. Instead, they are intent on deepening our understanding of the key issues concerning globalization. Their critical scrutiny ranges from the structure and strategies of the transnational music industries to an examination of the local and individual appropriation of global goods. They also discuss dissemination through migration and communities of interest, and the ideological and political use of different kinds of music. In addition, the book offers a valuable aid to future research in its accomplished presentation of theoretical models and methodologies for analyzing the globalization of music.

Professor Derek B. Scott
Chair of Music
University of Salford

Introduction

Andreas Gebesmair

Mediacult, the International Research Institute for Media, Communication and Cultural Development based in Vienna, organized a conference of experts on 'Music and Globalization' in Vienna from 4 to 6 November, 1999. The conference, which took place in the context of an ongoing research project at the institute, focused on the changing conditions of music production and distribution in a globalized world.

More and more cultural goods are produced for and distributed on the world market. This development is boosted by transnational culture industries which are not only seeking to reach increasingly larger markets but also appropriating the creative resources in different parts of the world. Facing these global strategies, the questions arise of how local and regional music cultures are affected by these strategies, if and under which conditions they can be sustained and which opportunities are given for a global dissemination of local music – *within* and *beyond* the major industry.

The papers presented at the conference were put together in this publication according to the distinction defined above. The articles in *Part I* are mainly concerned with the structure and strategies of the transnational music industry, whereas the articles in *Part II* widen their focus to aspects of globalization beyond that industry: the dissemination through migration and communities of interest, the local appropriation and the ideological and political use of different kinds of music. Furthermore, several approaches and methods of analyzing the globalization of music are presented in *Part III*.

Keeping in mind that the placement of each contribution within a chapter tends to be arbitrary and that there is no strong distinction between the three parts, the following introduction gives an overview of individual aspects of globalized music production by drawing on the articles in this publication. Names in italics refer to the authors of articles of this publication.

As expressed in the subtitle, this publication focuses on popular music. Without providing an exact definition, it should be mentioned that the articles are concerned neither with so-called classical music (in the occidental tradition) nor with traditional folk music. The music discussed later on is in one way or another connected to the rock aesthetic (Regev 1997) which has been in the center of the transnational music industry since the 1950s, although it may rely on aspects of traditional folk or classical music.

Structures and strategies of the transnational music and media industry

When discussing globalization it could be useful to begin with an analysis of the transnational music industry. This industry is the main force in global music distribution, deploying mass communication technologies, especially sound carriers, satellite broadcasting and the Internet, to reach markets all over the world. Like the development in other industrial areas, the process of globalization is accompanied by an extremely high concentration. Only five major companies hold about 80 percent of the world market. Furthermore, growing vertical and multimedia integration, as evidenced by the merger of Warner and AOL – a huge Internet provider – secures their high profits under changing technological circumstances.

Additionally, the major companies have at their disposal a global web of local subsidiaries and affiliated labels that serve as local distributors of their products as well as a pool for recruiting new artists. As Robert *Burnett* states in his contribution, competition between companies is being increasingly replaced by internal competition between subsidiaries trying to push their local artists into the global market. Thus Sweden, though a very small country, gained a strong position on the international market.

This example shows that the global repertoire of the major labels no longer represents the culture of a certain country but is fed by different sources. Whereas the industry follows the expansion logic of all capitalistic enterprises, the distribution of music can no longer be expressed in terms of 'cultural imperialism'. 'We can no longer sensibly define the international music market in nationalistic terms, with some countries (the USA, the UK) imposing their culture on others. This does not describe the cultural consequences of the new multinationals: whose culture do Sony-CBS and BMG-RCA represent?' (Frith 1991).

But how might we describe the culture of the transnational music industry? What is the so-called 'international repertoire' distributed on a world market and how does it sound? What criteria must it satisfy? Keith *Negus* refers to the international departments of major labels which develop a set of implicit criteria to evaluate music and artists. Through the aesthetic judgment of the international staff, a certain 'culture' has been established which has a high influence on local subsidiaries and hence on the production of music. To gain support from international departments, the music has to fit their standards which include a recognizably melodic structure, the ballad form, a voice without accent and a globally comprehensive image.

Nevertheless, the major labels also produce so-called 'local repertoire'. In order to satisfy local demands on different markets, the companies diversify their repertoire. In some countries the share of local repertoire is fairly high. While in some countries such as Austria and Canada the share does not exceed 15%, in others, like Japan, the UK, Brazil, or Russia, the domestic share accounts for more than 50% of the national markets. The category 'domestic share', however, does not necessarily mean that this music sounds unlike 'international repertoire' (see Andreas *Gebesmair*).

The effort to adjust the repertoire to regional markets has its limits in the media industry. Content analysis of regional MTV programs undertaken by Keith *Roe* and Gust *de Meyer* has shown that the regionalization of the media industry does not mean that programing is getting more 'regional'. Even though MTV-Europe abandoned English as their dominant language for moderation, little has changed in terms of the origins of artists and the language of the songs purveyed: Anglo-American and English repertoire is still predominant.

The global use and abuse of popular music – beyond the transnational music industry

The analysis of the music industry has shown the following: there is indeed a globally expanding ('imperialistic') music industry which seeks to distribute standardized products all over the world at high profits. But this industry has no identifiable cultural center: Their products do not represent the culture of a single country. Additionally, the industry considers local demands and produces local repertoire to satisfy this demand.

Yet there is a third argument for rejecting the 'cultural imperialism thesis': The dominance of the major industry and its repertoire does not mean that local culture has vanished. Beyond the interests of the majors, there are multiple ways of using international music. Describing the development of 'Austropop', Edward Larkey (1992) identified four different stages of the integration of international repertoire into local contexts: consumption, imitation of the imported music by local artists, de-Anglicization and re-ethnification. In this last stage, international repertoire merges with local traditions to form new genres which rely on different sources. This phenomenon of 'hybridization' caused by new communication technologies and global industries has struck all over the world since the seventies and eighties (Wallis and Malm 1984, Garofalo 1993, Taylor 1997) and has given rise to an abundance of new genres from Bhangra to Zouk, from Reggae to Rai, from Austro- to Turkpop. (See also the examples in the contributions of Alenka *Barber-Kersovan*, Susanne *Binas*, Deborah *Pacini Hernandez*, Harald *Huber*, Krister *Malm*, Ina *Zukrigl* and Joana *Breidenbach*.)

But what chance has this music to reach the ears of listeners beyond the immediate environment of its origin?

The record industry has of course recognized that there is a profitable global demand for music with local color. But this process has also been boosted by movements beyond the transnational music industry. In the eighties for instance, when many Dominicans began migrating to the USA, new markets emerged for the distribution of *meringue*, the Dominican Republic's most common genre of popular music. Deborah *Pacini Hernandez* argues that migration is a key but often under-appreciated aspect of globalization. Krister *Malm* also points to the translocation of persons rather than sound carriers. He reports of 'interlocal communities of interest' which exist beyond the transnational culture industry. Fans of Trinidad carnival music, soca and steel bands, have established a global web of mutual exchange which connects such distant countries as Sweden, Canada, and Trinidad. The Internet has proved to be an important device which supports this global exchange. Followers of the Syrian Orthodox Church living in diaspora all over the world created a virtual Syrian nation on the World Wide Web, which satisfies all prerequisites of a real nation from anthems to children's books.

But popular music, especially so-called 'domestic' repertoire, is also subject to political use and abuse. Music and the terms which denote it are used to strengthen ideological positions. Ideological content was transported for example in Serbian popular music production by relying on folk music elements, while Croatian music production avoided references to Balkan folk music by using international repertoire forms (Alenka *Barber-Kersovan*). More generally, Alfred *Smudits* shows that definitions of 'domestic repertoire' differ according to economic and political interests, just as ideologically biased marketing categories (like 'Latin music') represent a certain 'hegemonic' view which sometimes contrasts with the demands of ethnic minorities (see Deborah *Pacini Hernandez*).

Approaches and methods: Popular music research between 'production of culture' and 'anthropology'

Without regarding the wide range of different approaches and methods in the history of popular music research (see e.g. Shuker 1994, Negus 1996), I'd like to touch on some methodological aspects mentioned in the following articles.

As described above, two different research areas are connected in the analysis of the globalization of music. On the one hand, the transnational music industry, its worldwide structure and the resulting conditions of music production is concerned. On the other hand, the diversity of consumption and production on a local level is of great importance. Hence two different 'approaches' seem to converge in the study of global music production: one which concerns more the 'structural constraints' through which music is formed and one which looks at the daily routine of music activities and the production of 'meaning' in different cultures. Richard A. *Peterson*, Joana

Breidenbach and Ina *Zukrigl* give a short introduction to the basis of each approach, termed 'production of culture' and 'anthropology'. Rather than forming opposing research traditions, their merger provides some advantages for the study of globalization. Recent anthropology dealing with global cultural exchange (e.g. Appadurai 1990, Hannerz 1992) has considered the role of industry and technology. On the other hand, sociologists in the production-of-culture tradition take also modalities of consumption into account (Peterson 1994).

Though the articles in this publication represent a wide range of approaches and their authors employ different methods, I'd like to mention three aspects which could be considered a common thread running through the discussion.

First, the cultural development is seen neither as a product of solitary creators nor as an immediate consequence of social change. Creation and consumption of cultural goods are intermediated by a variety of relatively autonomous milieus or fields of production which deserve special scrutiny (Peterson 1976, Becker 1982, Bourdieu 1983). Keith *Negus* explains how popular music emerges from a complex and conflict-ridden process of bargaining between different actors within the music industry. Furthermore, the production process is constrained by a number of factors such as industry structure (Robert *Burnett*), marketing strategies (Keith *Roe* and Gust *de Meyer*, Deborah *Pacini Hernandez,* Richard A. *Peterson*), legal and political circumstances (Alenka *Barber-Kersovan*, Alfred *Smudits*) and, most prominently, technology (Susanne *Binas*, Krister *Malm*, Robert *Burnett*).

This production process does not end with the delivery of products but is extended to consumers who appropriate these cultural goods. In this sense we can regard reception too as a process where the meaning of culture is produced and sometimes reappropriated by the transnationals. (See the term 'autoproduction of culture' in Peterson 1994.)

Second, the research presented in this book relies on empirical research instead of a speculative and sometimes arbitrary search for 'traces of unconsciousness' or 'preferred readings' in musical texts. The methods range from the quantitative analysis of industry statistics to participant observation, from the qualitative interviews to style analysis. It is important to say that all these approaches rely on a kind of 'controlled observation' of reality and research is accompanied by a continuous discussion of reliability and validity of indicators (Andreas *Gebesmair*). Even the interpretation of musical texts is based on the analysis of different musical dimensions which has to be defined as exactly as possible (Harald *Huber*).

Third, the authors of these articles hesitate to demonize mass culture (as representatives of the Frankfurt School have done) as well as to romanticize creative subcultures (as Cultural Studies academics have done). As Simon Frith (1992) noted, the high affinity of some academics to youth culture and the resulting myth of resistance are more reflections of the situation of intellectuals than of the reality of young musicians. Therefore, a closer look at the meanings people attribute to cultural goods is indispensable in understanding different cultures. Anthropologists call for a so-called 'emic' perspective, or as Bronislaw Malinowski put it: The goal of ethnography is 'to grasp the native's point of view, his relation to life, to realize his vision of his world.' (See Joana *Breidenbach/*Ina *Zukrigl.*)

References

Appadurai, Arjun (1990). 'Disjuncture and Difference in the Global Cultural Economy.' *Theory, Culture & Society* Volume 7, 295–310.

Becker, Howard (1982). *Art worlds.* Berkeley Los Angeles London: University of California Press.

Bourdieu, Pierre (1983). 'The Field of Cultural Production, or: the Economic World Reversed.' *Poetics* 12, 311–356.

Frith, Simon (1991). 'Anglo-America and its Discontent.' In: Straw, Will and John Shepherd (eds). The Music Industry in a Changing World. *Cultural Studies* Volume 5/3, 263–269.

Frith, Simon (1992). 'The Cultural Study of Pop.' In: Grossberg, Lawrence, Cary Nelson and Paula Treichler (eds): *Cultural Studies.* New York London: Routledge.

Garofalo, Reebee (1993). 'Whose World, What Beat: The Transnational Music Industry, Identity, and Cultural Imperialism.' In: Erlmann, Veit and Deborah Pacini Hernandez (eds). The Politics and Aesthetics of 'World Music'. *The world of music* Volume 35(2), 16–32.

Hannerz, Ulf (1992). *Cultural Complexity.* New York: Columbia Univ. Press.

Larkey, Edward (1992). 'Austropop: popular music and national identity in Austria.' *Popular Music* 11 (2), 151–185.

Negus, Keith (1996). *Popular Music in Theory.* Hanover London: Wesleyan University Press.

Peterson, Richard A. (1976). 'The Production of Culture: A Prolegomenon.' *American Behavioral Scientist* Volume 19 No. 6, 669–684.

Peterson Richard A. (1994). 'Culture Studies Through the Production Perspective.' In: Crane, Diana (ed.). *The Sociology of Culture.* Cambridge, 163–189.

Regev, Matti (1997). 'Rock Aesthetics and Musics of the World.' *Theory, Culture & Society* Volume 14/3, 125–142.

Shuker, Roy (1994). *Understanding Popular Music.* London New York: Routledge.

Taylor, Timothy D. (1997). *Global Pop: World Music, World Markets.* New York: Routledge.

Wallis, Roger and Krister Malm (1984). *Big Sounds from Small Peoples: The Music Industry in small countries.* London: Constable.

Part I:
Structures and strategies of the transnational music and media industry

1 Global strategies and local markets: Explaining Swedish music export success

Robert Burnett

> 'In the electronic age we are all living by music.' *Marshall McLuhan*

The recent World Bank report, 'World Development Report 1999', describes the current 'state of the world' (according to the World Bank) and points out several key developments. Two trends dominate current economical, political and cultural development. The first and most well known and researched, is globalization. The other, much lesser known, is localization. Localization refers to the growing importance for regions, cities, and other entities beneath the national level. Both globalization and localization are described as inevitable, but with inherent risks and possibilities when it comes to different nations' ability to adapt and meet the challenge. Globalization may increase welfare while at the same time destabilizing certain nations. Localization may lead to increased democratic participation and influence as well as increasing tensions within certain countries. What I would now like to do in this paper is see how globalization and localization can be applied to our understanding of the music industry.

The global music industry

Music, its production, distribution, regulation and reception, is an essential feature of the European information society. The European music industry is a key asset. Today, two of the world's four largest music groups are European. The Bertelsmann Music Group (Germany), and EMI (UK, now controlled by AOL/Time Warner USA), together with Universal (Canada, formerly Polygram/MCA), and Sony (Japan) account for about 80% of the world market for pre-recorded music, a market that was worth an estimated 37 bn ECU in 1998. The music business also has many small companies. The fact that 60 percent of recordings sold in the EU originate in the EU means that local audiences are likely to continue to demand 'local' products despite the 'globalization' of the music industry. In Greece, the United Kingdom, France and Italy, the majority of records sold are by local artists. In the Scandinavian countries around 30 percent of all purchases are by local artists. In Austria and Belgium the number sinks to about 15 percent. Internationally, between 1991 and 1997 the percentage of the global music market share attained by European artists rose from 34 to 42 percent.

The four large multinational music companies operating in Europe are known as 'the transnationals, majors or multis', depending on where you live. Together, these four companies have about an 80 percent share of the global market. Some several thousand independent phonogram companies supply the remaining 20 percent of the market. Many of these are very small companies, some making only one or two releases a year. However, the independent companies are a very important part of the music industry since they are often at the leading edge of developments in popular music, with the ability to discover new talent and establish new trends. They also have to face the risks inherent in developing a new repertoire.

Universal, EMI, Sony, Warner and BMG all own and operate national distribution systems within the EU, distributing their own and third-party sound recordings to retailers, wholesalers and smaller distributors. Several of the majors also own and operate their own CD, cassette and vinyl-record manufacturing facilities.

As well as supplying phonograms nationally, the music companies exploit their recordings in foreign markets. Normally this is done by licensing a local company to supply phonograms in a particular country. In the case of the majors this is usually done through the music company's local affiliate. The independent phonogram companies often rely on unconnected companies to perform this function, including the majors' foreign affiliates. Licence income generated in this way is important to music companies. Europe is second to the United States as a supplier of recorded music to the rest of the world, but is closing the gap as more European artists gain global exposure.

The Internet and the music industry

The music business has often very little to do with music. It essentially consists of fast-moving, unit-led production, marketing, licensing and distribution functions. How much product will sell in which markets, how quickly they can ship, how fast they can restock, and so on. With the Internet as a potential high-speed digital distribution channel, phonogram companies will no longer be in a position to control the distribution chain. As a result they may be unable to shape the demand for a product. When music is distributed over the Internet, only one master copy is required. New artists who can create their own product will potentially be able to produce, market and distribute their work without the involvement of the major phonogram companies. This scenario is an example of *disintermediation* (cutting out the middle layers of certain distribution channels) in the extreme and would result in the collapse of the music business of today. However, it is an ideal that may never be fully realized. It disregards the possible actions that the key players in the multi-million ECU music business may take to reposition themselves in order to acquire a competitive edge in the changing conditions of the new Internet economy.

There are a number of complex technological and copyright issues that need to be resolved before the digital distribution of music can develop into a commercially viable product. For the foreseeable future, most consumers will continue to purchase hard copies of pre-recorded music, currently in the form of compact discs (CDs), mini discs, cassettes and vinyl records. These products can be purchased from a number of different sources including web shops, specialist music shops, supermarkets, gas stations and mail-order catalogues. During the 1990s, the Internet has been developed as a new medium for the exchange of information between businesses and consumers. It has the potential to enable merchants to incur lower costs in reaching consumers and supplying products, and to provide consumers with more choice and lower prices twenty-four hours a day, seven days a week. Although the amount of commerce conducted on the Web remains relatively small, its volume is increasing. Many companies are now looking into the possibility of on-line retailing.

The importance and implications of retailing on the Internet are likely to grow in the near future as technologies become more affordable and reliable, and as people become more aware of the potential efficiencies that can be achieved. Other benefits for organizations using the Internet as a retail outlet include the potential widening of their markets; better meeting of customer needs; faster introduction of innovative products and services; better customer-supplier interactivity; improved market intelligence, and lower costs and faster turnover. However, for coherent realization of these benefits, there are a number of fundamental changes that must take place, not only within organizations, but also in society at large. A number of improvements must be made: financial, legal and regulatory frameworks must be made clear and coherent, and security, privacy and authentication issues must be addressed, both at the practical level and in legislation.

The relatively minor cost of establishing home pages that offer goods or services attracts both existing merchants and newcomers. Theoretically, anyone who opens or accesses a Web site can enter the market. Merchants are able to gain direct access to consumers, thereby avoiding the need to go through various intermediaries to reach them. This may make it possible for them to avoid certain intermediary costs, such as distribution inventories and maintenance of expensive retail shops. Technically, the Web can be accessed from all over the world through the Internet. However, to become known and make a profit requires promotion, and in this respect established companies with well-known names and brands are in a better position than new entrants, who need significant capital to advertise. Nevertheless, in some respects, new entrants are in a more advantageous position than fully established companies, not only because of lower costs, but also because they may be better able to make quick changes in response to changes in consumer demand.

The possible entrants to the on-line music market are both large and small firms and include music store retailers, mail-order retailers, phonogram companies, broadcasters, and start-up enterprises with no previous experience in the music business. First movers often face disadvantages as well as advantages. Therefore it is strategically important for a company in considering whether to enter the on-line music market to understand the significance of the timing of market entry in relation to its competitors and the current state of advanced communication technologies and services.

Like other service industries, the music industry is repeatedly undergoing structural changes that are related to technological innovation. As the music industry is an innovation-intensive industry it warrants more attention especially as it incorporates advanced information and communication technologies more centrally into its core marketing practices.

Open production system

Due in part to the ever-increasing range of musical styles the transnationals have opted for a more 'open' system of production. This process is at work in Sweden as in most other countries. Multiple independent production units take care of artist and repertoire (A&R) and recording, while the 'parent' company takes care of manufacturing, marketing and distribution. This enables the transnationals to exploit both the talents of small creative units to identify potential successful new artists and sounds, as well as the advantages of large-scale manufacturing and distribution. In effect, the modern transnational phonogram company consists of many independently operating creative units at the 'input' side, and concentrated manufacturing and distribution at the 'output' side. To regulate the flow of products through the channels of a transnational, an internal market is at work in which the independent units act like they would in a more normal market. For example, Sony USA and Sony UK are in competition to have their products released in Sweden. This system of internal competition is coupled with a centralized control set-up that helps the local units to best deploy their resources. All creative units, at a national level, are allowed to try out new artists within their budget. Once a particular artist becomes successful in either a geographical region or within a specialized music genre, the combined resources are provided. That particular artist becomes a priority.

This partially explains how Garth Brooks and country music were a hit in Sweden in 1997, as well as why Ricky Martin and his Latino sounds were the summer of 1999 flavour in Sweden. As a consequence, the national units can concentrate their resources on this potentially successful artist, thereby increasing the chances of turning a local success into an international one.

The case of Sweden

The Swedish music industry is in one sense no longer Swedish because the transnationals essentially control the production, and distribution of popular music. During the eighties and nineties the transnationals bought up all the Swedish phonogram companies of significance. The only remaining Swedish labels are small, most of which have rosters of fewer than a dozen artists. The transnationals work in Sweden in much the same way they do in most other countries. The role of the transnationals in Sweden is now predominantly concerned with three major activities.

First, to ensure the local selling of international artists (a job previously licensed to Swedish companies).

Second, to ensure the local selling of local artists (a job previously done by Swedish companies).

Third, increasingly important is to develop local artists to plug into the international 'talent pool' (a job nobody did until recently).

Swedish popular music has in recent years risen to new heights of export success. From Abba, to Europe, Roxette, Ace of Base, and the Cardigans, to name the most prominent examples, the list of recent export successes goes on and on. Jonas Åkerlund is one of the hottest video producers these days and the services of the late music producer Denniz Pop and his partner Max Martin have long been sought after by international artists and record companies alike. This in turn has led to an interest in Sweden as a music nation. Where does the success come from? Why just Sweden? How much money does this success involve? Why is Swedish music considered so cool by so many?

Export earnings of the Swedish music industry

Previous attempts to measure the overseas earnings of the record industry have relied on estimates based on the known share of world sales accounted for by Swedish resident companies, artists and writers. In order to provide a more accurate assessment of recording-industry overseas earnings, Export

Music Sweden (ExMS), the International Federation of the Phonographic Industry (IFPI) Sweden, the Swedish Performing Rights Society (STIM), and the Swedish Artists' and Musicians' Interest Organisation (SAMI), undertook a survey of the overseas earnings of its largest members – estimated likely to account in total for over 90 percent of the industry's total overseas earnings – for the calendar years 1994, 1995, 1996 and 1997. Record companies were asked to provide details of earnings received from overseas for the corresponding periods. The companies responding were Polygram, Stockholm Label Group, Sony, BMG, Warner, EMI, MCA, Virgin, MNW, and Arcade. Wherever possible the survey figures for individual companies were verified against the detailed published accounts made available by some companies.

While the figures presented in Table 1.1 seem substantial, we know that they are on the conservative side; a number of major Swedish artists receive their royalty income from overseas recordings directly rather than through their Swedish recording company. Many artists categorized as Swedish also live or are registered abroad and total royalties repatriated will only be a portion of the total. In many cases, publishing, record company and other incomes from sales by Swedish artists also do not return to Sweden. 'Swedish' albums on major labels selling in Germany could be recorded in the UK, published in the US and manufactured and distributed in Germany. For example, artists such as Ace of Base, Neneh Cherry, Dr. Alban and Wannadies are all signed to foreign labels and as such earn no money in Sweden.

What is interesting to note is that the export of Swedish music is not confined to a small group of artists but shows a breadth of talent when it comes to music companies, music styles, artists and producers. Bearing in mind the factors mentioned relating to interpreting the export trade data, the record industry generated significant income, which is presented in Table 1.1 under Recordings.

Music publishing

Music-publishing overseas earnings are generated from one of three main sources: First, direct receipts from Swedish Music Publishers Association/ Svenska Musikförläggareföreningen (SMFF) promoting copyrighted musical works overseas who are foreign music publishing affiliates, sub-publishers and exclusive and non-exclusive agents for Swedish companies. This income was estimated at approximately 200 million SEK per annum and is shown in Table 1.1 under Music publishers. Second, through income collected by the Performing Rights Society/Svenska tonsättares internationella musikbyrå (STIM) from overseas affiliated societies for broadcast and public performances abroad. Third, through the Nordisk Copyright Bureau (NCB) which receives certain mechanical rights income from overseas. The money collected by STIM for radio and TV broadcast and public performance of Swedish music in foreign countries together with the money collected by NCB for mechanical rights are presented in Table 1.1 under Copyright/Composers/Publishers.

Copyright income to artists/musicians

The Swedish Artists and Musicians Interest Organisation (SAMI) collects money for its members from countries that have signed the Rome Convention on copyrights. This money is from the radio and TV broadcast of Swedish music and from the public broadcasting of recordings (for example, airports, restaurants, and shopping malls). Copyright income collected by SAMI is presented in Table 1.1 under Musicians/Artists.

Performance income

The area of performance-related income – in this case individuals and groups undertaking engagements or promotions overseas – is arguably the most difficult sub-sector of the music industry to measure. There is little doubt that, in theory, there should be considerable net inflows of income arising from foreign touring by Swedish artists. It is well known that, for established acts, very substantial sums can be generated from ticket sales and associated merchandising. Historically, tours had been valued more for their promotional qualities: their use in drawing a public's attention to new albums and as a means of exposing young acts. More recently there has been greater emphasis on direct income generation from major international tours facilitated in part by commercial sponsorship tie-ins, relatively high ticket prices and a seemingly strong demand. Information on the gross earnings of tours in the US and Canada are published in the trade press and these data confirm the considerable sums involved.

However, several issues arise when making a reasonable estimate of Swedish earnings from overseas appearances. First, while gross earnings from overseas touring may be substantial, it is often uncertain what element of touring income returns to Sweden; some artists accrue financial advantage by being based 'off-shore'. Second, this area, probably more than any other element of overseas earnings in music, is likely to be affected by substantial year-to-year variations. Clearly, however, major overseas tours by Swedish acts do result in some flow back of funds. Some tours actually lose money!

An estimate of the total earnings of Swedish resident artists and acts from overseas performances is not easy. It is important to openly acknowledge that this particular area of overseas music activity is liable to a high level of estimation and error.

The Swedish Promoters Organisation (SVIMP) has estimated that a reasonable figure would be around 200 million SEK per year. I see no reason to question this figure and use it as an annual estimation of performance income for Swedish artists touring abroad, which is presented in Table 1.1 as Performance income.

Summary of export earnings

This report brings together a range of data on the overseas earnings of the Swedish music industry. It has benefited considerably from a number of new surveys, which have reduced the degree of estimation in earlier and more broadly based estimates of the music sector's earnings abroad. The summary data is presented in Table 1.1:

Table 1.1 Export earnings of the Swedish music industry

Amounts in SEK million (1 US$ = 8 SEK)	1994	1995	1996	1997
Recordings	876	914	1,272	1,167
Copyright				
Composers/Publishers	306	331	413	433
Musicians/Artists	17	17	19	21
Music publishers	200	200	200	200
Performance income	200	200	200	200
Total	1,599	1,662	2,104	2,021

Overall the overseas earnings of the music industry were estimated to fluctuate from 1.6 billion SEK in 1994, to a high of 2.1 billion SEK in 1996. In each of those categories where figures have been compiled for overseas earnings (recording, music publishing, live performance) the data point to sizeable earnings. The music industry is a substantial earner of foreign exchange for the Swedish economy.

No study of a sector as complex as the music industry can ever be entirely complete and there are areas where we have had to resort to estimates. But with one exception – the overseas earnings of artists – the sectors where estimates are used are small. All other areas are based on survey results, official statistics, company accounts and other information. The largest areas are based on statistical surveys or official data. When estimates are used the policy has been conservative in order to avoid any possibility of inflating the results.

Explaining the success

What are the reasons behind the export success of Swedish pop music? Are there explanatory factors that are theoretically feasible and that make practical sense? What follows are the explanatory clusters that arose from the research into Swedish music export.

The first factor revolves around musical competence. Sweden has a tradition of well-developed municipal music schools. The schools provide youth training in song, on instruments, and to some extent composing and mixing skills. The music schools are essentially free for students as they are operated and funded by the local municipalities. At present there are 370,000 children in training at the 286 music schools in Sweden, at a total cost of 1.3 million SEK (Finansdepartementet 1999). Essentially, any children who want to learn to sing or play an instrument are provided with the opportunity to do so.

There are also a series of special music classes where children get an extra dose of music on the curriculum. The amount of space in these special classes is limited, so there is a great deal of competition involved. Not all municipalities provide special music classes.

Many successful Swedish artists had their initial music training in the special music classes and especially the municipal music schools. There is little doubt that this broad training has resulted in the emergence of talent. There are of course special music high schools and music training at the university level, but this is also relatively common in many countries.

A second cluster relates to the structure of the Swedish music industry. All the transnational music companies are represented with their subsidiaries, and there is a large group of independent companies. There are several internationally established recording studios with sought after engineers and producers. There are also large publishing houses, both domestic and international. There is a wealth of actors in all sectors of the music industry, thus reinforcing each other and creating competitive advantages. It takes this industrial competitiveness, several firms that are both competing and co-operating with each other, to trigger industry growth.

A third cluster involves the networks of interorganizational links, voluntary associations, and service organizations. The various actors in the music business, whether they be firms or individual artists, composers, music teachers, publishers, etc., appear to have a high capacity for self-organization, and are able to create mechanisms for co-ordination to promote joint interests, to exchange information and to act together.

A fourth cluster has to do with the Swedish audience. Swedish listeners are a rather demanding and internationally oriented audience. Swedish contemporary pop music is often written and performed in English, hence Swedish artists have immediate access to the most important global pop music markets. A total of 400,000 out of a population of just under 9 million sing in choirs and are competent readers of music. There is also an abundance of quality music instruments in Swedish homes. A sophisticated audience is generally acknowledged as an important factor in maintaining the competitiveness of an industry.

Conclusion

When it comes to the music industry I think that one can say that globalization and localization are of some use to us in theory building. One would be unwise to focus upon one aspect at the expense of the other. What has the move towards globalization and localization meant for the Swedish music industry?

Swedish popular music has developed into a highly competitive export industry. A growing number of artists have made it big on the global music scene. The best known examples are ABBA in the 1970s, Europe in the 1980s, and Roxette, Ace of Base and the Cardigans in the 1990s. According to recent studies (Burnett 1997; 1999) annual Swedish net exports of popular music rose to 2.1 billion SEK in the mid 1990s. This makes Sweden one of the largest net exporters of popular music, after the US and the UK. Not only Swedish artists have been successful. Music producers such as the late Denniz Pop, Max Martin, Douglas Carr, Tore Johansson, and video director Jonas Åkerlund have become successful and much in demand internationally.

The strength of the Swedish music industry rests on the creative talent of Swedish composers, performers and lyricists allied to the business skills of music companies and entrepreneurs. A range of factors is believed by those in the industry to have helped the flow of consistent creative talent which enables Sweden to produce performers who can compete in the global marketplace. Music classes in elementary school, municipal music schools, and music facilities for youth are often mentioned as helping to produce a fund of talented performers in all areas of music making. Immigration and the music that follows in its path is another possible factor, as is the relatively high-level access to music instruments and recording equipment. Sweden's strengths in music-making have resulted not only in a lively and diverse cultural scene but also in significant economic success.

References

Burnett, Robert (1996). Swedish Music Industry Survey.
Burnett, Robert (1996). *The Global Jukebox: The International Music Industry.* London/New York: Routledge.
Burnett, Robert (1997). Den svenska musikindustrins export 1994–95.
Burnett, Robert (1998). Den svenska musikindustrins export 1996–97.
Burnett, Robert (1999). 'Phonograms.' In: *Media Sweden 1999.* Gothenburg: Nordicom.
Finansdepartementet (1999). Att ta sig ton – om svensk musikexport 1974–1999. Ms 1999: 28.
IFPI Musik på fonogram: 1994/1995/1996/1997/1998.
STIM Annual Reports: 1994/1995/1996/1997/1998.
World Bank (1999) World Development Report 1999.

2 The corporate strategies of the major record labels and the international imperative

Keith Negus

According to the division of labor for this book, I have been asked to discuss corporate maneuverings as they pertain to the 'inner' organization of the music industry[1]. Such a task involves drawing an analytic boundary around social processes that are not so neatly contained. Hence, I should stress at the outset that the internal organizational dynamics of music companies I am discussing here are continually shaped by a set of relationship to the external world. The music industry is more than a site of production. It is a corporate space within which various people attempt to manage the often fragmentary social relationships through which music is produced, consumed and given meaning. In the process recording corporations use a number of explicit strategies in an attempt to connect the 'inside' of production (which is increasingly outside of a company with artists, producers and arrangers) to the 'outside' of consumption (which is increasingly brought in to the company through various techniques of monitoring and information production). Corporate strategy is central to any consideration of musical mediation as it entails an explicit attempt to manage the production-consumption relationship of music, and it is this relationship (or the frequent lack of relationship or coherent 'fit' between the two sides) which produces so much uncertainty, anxiety, conflict and confusion.

Given my brief for this contribution, however, and due to the space available, I shall confine myself to an outline of some of the key structures and strategies which tell of the practices of the major record labels. In addition, bearing in mind that this book is about music and globalization, I shall also do my best to avoid straying into areas that might duplicate the thematic focus of other contributions in this collection.

Multinational corporations

My focus is on the 'major' record labels of the multinational entertainment companies, and I follow those numerous writers who have stressed the importance and influence exerted by multinational corporations. Whilst numerous record companies may have started as small operations, based in one location, run in a 'family'-like manner, throughout the twentieth century the major labels have developed as multi-divisional companies and then into complex conglomerate groupings (tied into other entertainment, leisure, media and manufacturing interests).

Of course, multinationals do not simply impose their will, and can be challenged in various ways. But, in general, the fates and fortunes of entrepreneurs and small and medium-sized enterprises ('independents') have to be realized *in relation* to the operations of the big conglomerates. This is apparent if we consider media ownership and cultural production in general. As has been well documented, a few large corporations (such as BMG, Sony, Disney, Universal, News International) account for the distribution of nearly all the top selling books, films, magazines and musical recordings (the products that generate the most revenue). Although many small companies also produce novels, films and music, these do not usually sell in such vast quantities. If such products receive critical acclaim, social recognition and, most significantly, go on to become commercially successful, then the small producer may well be courted by the multinational. Indeed, for many years, the dynamics of cultural production have been characterized by a continual process of acquisitions, financing and deal making between small and large companies which usually results in the small company becoming an operating unit of the large corporation (or key personnel moving over to the large corporation).

It is important to stress that the influence of the multinational corporations (MNCs) is not one of outright domination of markets. As a number of researchers have found, in many parts of the world there are, quantitatively, far more locally produced films, musical recordings and television programs being made, circulated and broadcast. However, these are not usually generating the same amount of revenue as the products distributed by the MNCs, nor are these local producers able to exert the same kind of influence over viewing and listening habits, buying patterns and the professional judgments of production and marketing executives. The influence of MNCs is often felt more strongly within the local offices of the corporation and its affiliates, than amongst consumers, and experienced in terms of the pressure to conform to a series of aesthetic and commercial agendas, working practices, production routines and working codes.

This pressure can be exerted in various ways. Like multi-divisional corporations in general, senior music industry management employ techniques of remote judging, dividing the company into a series of strategic business units, and using various economic indicators as a means of judging the 'efficiency', performance and profile of each unit. Accounting knowledge has emerged as the particular way of ordering and assessing the actions of individuals within multi-divisional corporations. It provides a way of privileging 'hard' data (facts, figures, statistics) over 'soft' explanations (human foibles, intuitive hunches and 'belief in an artist').

Structures and strategies

Hence, my first and probably obvious point, is that record companies are structured into a series of business units that are judged according to clearly defined economic criteria of success/failure (budgets, profits, return on investment, market share figures). There are three significant additional ways that companies are structured. First, the corporation divides staff according to specific occupational tasks; into discrete departments such as A & R (artists & repertoire), marketing, radio promotion, business affairs and so on. Second, they divide staff according to genre/music style (country, jazz, classical, dance, etc), partly in an attempt to overcome the occupational divisions which so often lead to conflicts between A & R (responsible for finding the new repertoire) and marketing (responsible for selling the new repertoire). Third, they divide staff according to specific notions of geographical territories. These are directly related to national and pan-national political institutional structures and 'markets' (i.e. the nation-state, regional [Latin America or EU] or 'global') and notions of what constitutes a 'domestic' sound and an 'international' sound.

These 'structures' are informed by strategy. One of the most obvious ways that record company strategy attempts to resolve the problem of production and consumption is through the organization of catalogues, departments and promotional systems according to genre categories. As Simon Frith has noted, in his book *Performing Rites* (Oxford, 1996), genre provides a way of linking the question of music (what does it sound like?) to the question of its market (who will buy it?). Hence, the separation of staff into discrete units to work r'n'b, rock, dance, country, enka, classical and so on. Record companies use the vocabulary of portfolio management when viewing the mix of their labels, genres and artists and as a means of assessing or characterizing the 'assets' in their portfolio (and when judging the investment required and the performance, profile and contribution of each).

In many ways this is part of a strategy of diversification; the company spreading its risks across various musical genres and potential sources of income. But, it is more than diversification. Portfolio management provides a way of managing the company's diverse range of interests, as each unit can be assessed and categorized according to its performance, artistic peculiarities and level of investment required.

Although using the terminology of business management, record companies use techniques which can be traced back throughout the reorganization of music catalogues which has occurred since late in the nineteenth century. This provides the company with a means of dividing up talent and structuring such a division into the corporate world. The following is something of an ideal type sketch of the criteria mobilized by companies when dividing up and categorizing their staff and artists.

Stars require substantial investment but their profile and market dominance enables the production of profits to finance further acquisitions and expansion. The delivery of albums from star artists can significantly affect a company's turnover and market share. But, stars need sophisticated management, experienced staff and personal attention (as Warner's dispute with Prince and Sony's court case with George Michael would seem to confirm). Such arrangements can be costly, as can the financial terms under which a star is kept under contract (e.g. Warners invested a huge amount in keeping REM at the company, and some commentators have suggested that the now three piece may not recoup the amount that the label have spent in trying to keep them at the corporation). Although stars may not necessarily provide the best cash flow, particularly when between albums, they may attract further investment, prestige and can draw other artists to a company.

Cash cows can produce sizable profits and with minor modifications and modest ongoing investment, this category can bring in regular revenue and maintain the company's market share. Cash cows can be managed with a fairly straightforward administrative structure and standard promotional system. When I interviewed one senior record company executive in London during November 1995 he remarked that for his company 'techno is really a cash cow'. Likewise, when speaking to staff in the United States during 1996, I routinely heard the category of 'alternative rock' spoken of as a cash cow.

Wild cat or question mark In the music business this label refers to a new genre (or, in certain cases, an artist) that the company may wish to become involved with so as to increase market interests and to broaden experience and expertise. Any potential commercial success may be difficult to predict and the company will probably need to invest in staff, artists, offices, equipment, and a catalogue before obtaining a significant return on any such investment.

Dogs produce little, if any, profit and are usually considered a bad investment. A company may wish to divest of a genre or artist defined as a 'dog'. However, record companies may retain a dog for reasons other than immediate financial gain. This has sometimes been the case with more experimental or avant garde performers and with classical music and jazz. This practice can benefit a company, both internally and externally. Such a strategy can impress and attract other artists and it can boost the morale of personnel within the company. It can be used to justify the claim that the company is interested in 'art' as much as profits (although such a strategy can also have indirect commercial benefits).

The practice of portfolio management enables the company to assess and divide up different genre divisions, labels or those working specific artists. It allows for particular techniques of monitoring which operate to enforce a high degree of accountability within the operating units. Each unit has to report regularly to corporate headquarters and has sales targets to hit, budgets to work within, and is rewarded for good performance and can be punished for poor performance. The company can reward for contributions to profile and profitability by allocating finance for expansion and by giving performance related bonuses. At the same time, the company can deploy sanctions for poor performances. Punishment can involve the sacking of individual senior executives and bringing in new presidents or it can involve the closing down of entire divisions and their removal from the company's portfolio (an occurrence which occurs with cyclical regularity in the recording industry).

These judgments also impact upon artists and staff working with artists – it is sometimes a short step from being labeled a dog and becoming a cash cow. This is (schematically) the context within which genres, artists, and staff struggle for position – this, at least formally, 'prior' to any attempt at 'global' marketing.

The international imperative

In certain respects, all this 'rationalization' occurs for the simple reason that none of the major music and media corporations have limitless sources of funds. They therefore allocate resources by establishing a series of commercial criteria and aesthetic hierarchies and use these to allocate greater investment to certain genres, artists, projects, songs and not others. When seeking talent and whether involved in finding and financing the production of films, books, recorded music, television programs, musicals, magazines or academic textbooks, greater investment will be accorded to those products judged to produce the greatest return on investment. When these judgments are made, what is euphemistically called the 'international potential' of any new film, singer, or novel is of paramount importance, and will influence who and what is acquired and the drawing up of contracts.

The so-called 'promotion' to an 'international market' appeals to record companies as much as it does to Hollywood film producers and to those making deals at the Frankfurt book fair. International sales can provide the corporation (and musicians) with extra income for proportionately less additional investment in production costs. Once initial investment has been recovered the cost of reproducing and distributing additional copies of films, novels or CDs is relatively low compared to the extra revenue that can be generated.

It is due to this sort of imperative that the international marketing department has come to assume an important position and become separated from other departments within the major labels. Drawn ever closer to corporate headquarters, and in some companies working within the remit of corporate head office, staff within the international marketing departments of the major labels have become the experts with whom those in a national territory (e.g. Japanese domestic) or label division (e.g. country music) must liaise and rely upon for knowledge, guidance and admission to 'global' markets. The status and influence of the international marketing department has increased since the late 1980s (the epoch when the major labels began deploying discourses of 'globalization' as a way of 're-imagining' the world).

Here, strategy, structure and culture collide as the international marketing staff assess and draw up a list of artists who will receive privileged investment for international promotion. Although this is an 'internal' bureaucratic procedure within the corporation, it is crucially connected to perceptions of the world outside the executive suite, and the judgments made are, in turn, based on a series of very specific cultural experiences. For, despite the numerous references to the term within business more generally, there are not simply 'global markets' waiting out there on the planet or spontaneously forming as members of the public gravitate towards certain artifacts and not others. The 'global market' is an idea that is constructed in a specific way by the music business (and made up in a contrasting but similar manner by other industries). Staff in the major record labels have adopted a particular way of understanding what global markets are, producing knowledge about them, and distributing that knowledge within the corporation.

Re-imaging the world as global and the global repertoire

In re-imaging the world for 'global marketing', Senior executives in the major corporations have adopted a particular way of understanding what 'global markets' are and draw upon a taken-for-granted reservoir of knowledge and a distinct set of experiences when making assessments about the world of music. This includes a series of very particular judgments (as a means of valuing music and performing artists):

1. Aesthetic judgments about the instruments, tempos, rhythms, voices and melodies that are able to 'travel well'. Semiotic judgments about the type of images – faces, bodies, clothing styles – that are considered more suitable for an 'international audience'.
2. Political judgments about areas of the world considered to be 'unstable' or where certain types of music are banned for moral or religious reasons.
3. Economic judgments about the number of potential consumers who can be reached and assessments about parts of the world where the corporation may have difficulty collecting revenue.
4. Marketing judgments about the arrangements for the distribution of recordings (the availability of radio, retail outlets, television broadcasting) and the 'penetration' of the technologies of musical reproduction (tape machines and CD players).

5. Financial legal judgments about the existence of copyright law that will ensure that recordings broadcast by the media, played in public and circulated for purchase, will generate rights revenue that will accrue to the corporation. Hence, the so-called 'global markets' tend to be those which have strictly enforced copyright legislation and highly priced CDs rather than cheaply priced cassettes (so Japan is an important global market, whereas India is not).

In this way the 'global' is imagined in terms of a series of very particular criteria, judgments that clearly depend upon very particular experience of and perception of the world. These criteria become focused on the aesthetic-commercial assessment of music as international repertoire, a category which has gained increasing currency and usage in the organizational discourses of the recording industry since the middle of the 1980s. It is a term used regularly by personnel within the music business, reported in trade reports and corporate publications and frequently found employed in record stores in non-English speaking countries. International repertoire is marketed to a 'global' market; the recordings are released simultaneously in all of the major territories of the world.

The category of international repertoire can be contrasted with 'regional repertoire', recordings that are released in a broad area (such as Spanish language popular music in Latin America or Mandarin pop in east Asia), and 'domestic repertoire', recordings released solely in one national territory. In practical terms international repertoire refers to a list of very specific artists. Staff in the international department at each major company, in collaboration with senior business affairs executives, have been accorded the task of drawing up a 'global' priority list of about 15 to 20 artists and advising other sections of the company if their artists are going to be admitted or not.

What guides the judgments that are made? How do staff decide which artists to admit and who to exclude? These were the sort of questions I sought to answer when I carried out research in Britain and the United States in the mid-1990s. The most obvious immediate answer is that this question is resolved according to economic criteria. It is those artists who have previously achieved international success and who are releasing a new album that will have little difficulty attracting radio play, media coverage and gaining sales. After this, it is those artists who have already achieved success in a specific part of the world and who seem likely to be able to 'break out' from a territory. However, such spontaneous breaking is subject to considerable rationalization and ordering. It is also subject to the imposition of a number of very particular aesthetic codes and cultural judgments prior to any attempt at promotion. There are, after all, at any one moment, many artists with the potential to 'internationalize'. Here musical criteria and aesthetic judgments play an important part when senior staff are deciding who is to be prioritized.

In February 1996 I interviewed David McDonagh, Senior VP of International at PolyGram's New York office and I asked him how he assessed acts for international priority. Like other international staff I have spoken to, he identified a very particular type of music. Knowing that I was particularly interested in the production of rap music, he explained his reasoning as follows:

> The basic kind of music that has broad appeal internationally is kind of like pop music ballads. Ballads always work. It doesn't matter if it's Whitney Houston, Mariah Carey, Bon Jovi or whoever it happens to be. A ballad is always going to be something that will work in basically every country around the world. So, with hip hop or rap music there aren't too many artists that have ballads. So, already you're in a situation where what fundamentally is going to work anywhere doesn't happen too often as far as hip hop and rap is concerned . . . Occasionally a song comes along that basically can be seen as a pop song in terms of having that immediate type of appeal and it's still by a rap or a hip hop artist but it just so happens that it's a song that has broader appeal. Warren G is an example with 'Regulate' which was like a sort of soft melodic type of song and it did have rapping throughout. It also happened to have a sample that was instantly recognizable . . . We currently have one song by LL Cool J which has Boyz 2 Men on it which is called 'Hey Lover' and that one is pretty much a ballad and because it features Boys 2 Men and that immediately gives it more of a pop feel.

David, like a number of people I interviewed, considered the rap tracks that had international appeal to be those which in aesthetic terms could be related to a slow ballad structure or which contained a highly distinctive melodic sample. Hence, 'Gangsta's Paradise' owed its success and international promotion as much to Stevie Wonder's heavily sampled slow melodic ballad 'Pastime Paradise' as it did to Coolio's rap, and, of course, its circulation on the 'Dangerous Minds' film soundtrack album. In a similar way, the international success enjoyed by Sean 'Puff Daddy' Combs might be explained in terms of his ability to transform ballads into rap tracks whilst retaining their recognizably melodic structure, as he did successfully in re-signifying the Police's 'Every Breath You Take' into 'I'll Be Missing You'.

It is these types of sounds which the major labels will be more inclined to invest time and money in promoting internationally and this has led to accusations that certain artists have recognized this and are wilfully sampling melodic songs and adding a small rap as a way of gaining wider promotion. Whilst there may be an element of truth in this claim (a pattern that was reproduced in the promotion of the track and film 'Wild, Wild, West', with Will Smith rapping over yet another track from Stevie Wonder's 'Songs in the Key of Life'), the dynamics driving the changing aesthetic style of rap are far more complicated and informed as much by the blurring of boundaries between soul, r' n 'b, jazz and rap as they are likely to be driven by any short-term ploy to make a fast buck.

In addition to providing music that in some way can be likened to a melodic ballad, any potential international artist must sing their ballads or melodic rock songs with the right kind of voice. This was highlighted by an international director who remarked that in theory an artist could come from any place in the world as long as they sing 'in English without an accent'.

The voice and language is crucial particularly when consideration is being given to artists who may have achieved considerable domestic or regional sales and who may be given the opportunity to 'have a shot' at the international market. This is a common career strategy that is built into the marketing plans of artists whose first language is English. The aim is to move a performer from 'domestic' (Britain, for example) to 'regional' (Europe) to 'international' (the rest of the world and, if coming from Britain, to the United States).

The problems of language and accent are not simply faced by artists whose first language is not English. Language and accent also present barriers to artists from the United States who may not be prioritized due to such judgments. Most notably, rap and country artists rarely make it into the international category. According to international marketing staff I have spoken to in the United States, Britain and Japan, both rap and country are judged to be 'too dependent upon the lyrics' or 'the vocals' and are considered to foreground the voice and lyrical content in a way that people from other parts of the world 'can't relate to' or 'cannot identify with'. Despite being heard around the world, a judgment is made that the vocal and musical accents of rap and country are too distinct for international priority and promotion (and the concomitant investment involved). Ironically, many British artists are not considered to have the requisite 'global English' accent to join the international category and since the early 1960s many British artists who have succeeded in the United States have done so singing with an 'American' inflexion and pronunciation to their singing.

The influence of international agenda

I should perhaps stress that international repertoire does not simply 'dominate' markets around the world. As mentioned above, the influence of international repertoire is often felt in terms of its adoption as a musical label which sets an agenda for other personnel within the company who wish to have their artists admitted to this category. Just as performers in Nashville, for example, can attempt to tailor their recordings to suit the requirements of country music radio, so artists and their representatives within various sections of the major corporations attempt to make subtle and not so subtle changes in an attempt to be placed on the international priority list. In this way international repertoire begins to function as a set of stylistic character-istics or a genre label within the corporation.

Rather than individual labels and departments approaching international staff with artists, the international division conducts a surveillance operation and places pressure on departments to 'think internationally' from the begin-ning. Rather than attempting to promote a diversity of existing artists, an ap-proach is adopted that involves locating artists who fit the criteria (and ignoring those who do not fit this formula). Staff begin to 'know' who should and should not be admitted. Word filters throughout the companies and is formally passed down to artist and repertoire staff: 'The artists who will gain most success are those with "international appeal"'.

Whilst musicians may well be inspired to adopt the characteristics of a particular musical style, it can be economically advantageous to be labeled in one way and not another. Being admitted to the category of international rep-ertoire will result in increased financial investment. In the long term, if lead-ing to success, it could mean admittance to an exclusive artist aristocracy. An artist prioritized for international promotion by a major record label is mar-keted and presented in a systematic way that involves the identification of key markets, the strategic geographical movement through these places and the support of a large promotional budget. The company establishes a clearly defined marketing plan, invests accordingly and promotes systematically through various targeted regional media. Staff in each regional office (whether Germany, Argentina, Japan or Australia) are given clear sales targets that they are expected to reach.

This can create a considerable amount of local frustration and tension, as staff in other territories often prefer to be working with their own artists than with a prioritized US or UK artist. Whatever the perceptions of markets held by local staff, regardless of their commitment to their own artists and despite personal preferences that may predispose them to certain performers and not others, these personnel must ensure that attention is first devoted to the world-wide priorities.

The international marketing department, drawn ever closer to the strategic planning staff at corporate head office, have ways of ensuring that these plans are implemented. One technique entails offering incentives: performance re-lated bonuses are awarded for exceeding sales targets, increasing market share and achieving high chart positions. At the same time, staff are routinely made accountable for not reaching established goals. The most common sanction is straightforward demotion or the termination of employment (the same consequence of not achieving specific goals in any record label divi-sion). Corporate headquarters also attempt to 'motivate' local staff in differ-ent territories by gaining their involvement in more subtle ways by offering access to artists, both backstage at events and in company offices.

In this way the success of a Mariah Carey, Elton John, Bon Jovi or Michael Jackson is prioritized and systematically implemented by the major company. Not only does this procedure entail the use of considerable financial resources, it involves a particular type of economic oriented, instrumental rationality. The diversity of musical activity in the world is reduced to a specific type of 'market' activity and a coercive management practice is deployed to enforce people, spread out in different offices around the world, to work in a particular way to ensure that international priorities do become successful. This is by no means the only dynamic or pressure force driving the global distribution of popular music, but it is a major dynamic and powerful influence, exerting considerable pressure within the music industry, and shaping the contexts within which musicians can realize their creative aims.

Note

1   I have intentionally kept this paper free of numerous scholarly footnotes. Those wishing to follow up the points made here should consult the more detailed discussion found in my book *Music Genres and Corporate Cultures*, Routledge 1999.

3 One Planet – One Music? MTV and globalization*

Keith Roe and Gust de Meyer

Introduction

Today, MTV can be viewed wherever satellite-TV reception is possible suggesting that it has fulfilled its early goal of becoming the world's first truly global network. However, it is not just because of its global character (which it shares e.g. with CNN) that MTV is important. MTV is also special because it claims to be different from other channels in being based on a completely new concept of television and the viewer, a concept based on the assumption that a certain type of content appeals universally to young people everywhere. The purpose of this paper is, in various ways, to examine this assumption. First, the origins, concept and development of MTV will be traced. Then, using the specific example of MTV-Europe, the extent to which cultural diversity has confronted and constrained MTV's global aspirations will be assessed. Finally, in the light of MTV's experiences, the concept of globalization itself will be critically examined.

The development of MTV

MTV made its debut on August 1, 1981 on 225 cable systems reaching 2.1 million households in the USA. Its first ever video clip, 'Video Killed The Radio Star' by the Buggles, was clearly intended to be prophetic. By the end of 1983 the channel was available to 18 million American households and, as the number of viewers rose, so did advertising revenue with the result that, after heavy losses in the first two years, MTV became profitable in 1984. By 1985, it was reportedly earning a profit of $ 31 million from revenues of $ 96 million (Montavalli 1986; Denisoff 1988; Banks 1996).

In 1987 MTV moved across the Atlantic, although it was not the first Music Video Channel to appear on European cable systems, this distinction being held by the short-lived 'Music Box'. Moves into Eastern Europe (1989), Latin America (1990), Japan (1992), Asia (1995) and Australasia (1997) soon followed, so that by 1995 MTV could claim to reach 320 million households in 90 countries on 5 continents, 24 hours a day (Burnett, 1996), thus fulfilling its early marketing slogan of 'One Planet One Music'.

In the early 1990s MTV was the fastest growing cable and satellite chan-nel in Europe, with distribution growing from 2.2 million households in 1987, through 20 million in 1990, to 56 million in 1996 (Bekaert, 1998a). Initially, the general format of MTV-Europe copied that of the parent Ameri-can station. Later, however, this was perceived to be a mistake (see Roe & Wallis 1989; Burnett 1990) and efforts were made to adapt its content and style to the European context.

The concept of music television

According to one of its creators, Robert W. Pittman (1990), MTV was specif-ically conceived and designed for the generation of 'TV babies' because, having grown up with television, they communicate, process information, and form ideas in ways different from those of their parents. Pittman argued that, while the latter are 'the one thing at a time' generation, the 'TV babies' by contrast, 'really can do their homework, watch television, talk on the phone and listen to the radio all at the same time'; simultaneously processing information from each source into a different cluster of thoughts. Moreover, he observed, they seem to perceive visual messages better and they can 'read' a picture and understand body language at a glance. The task for television makers, he concluded, was to learn to speak the language of this television generation.

After extensive market research the grammar of this 'new language' was seen as the integration of television and rock music in the now well-estab-lished music video clip format. As Hartman (1987: 19) pointed out, this po-tent mix had long been used in TV commercials (and, more recently, in longer music videos), 'but not in as dynamic a fashion and not with such spectacular results as MTV achieved in penetrating the youth and young-adult market'. Moreover, such an integration promised solutions to perceived problems in both the television and the music industry. At that time, contem-porary music radio was losing its audience (Straw 1988), the recording in-dustry was in a recession (Burnett 1990), and TV producers had always been comparatively unsuccessful in reaching the notoriously elusive 12–34 age segment.

The basic original format of MTV was based on that of Top 40 radio pro-gramming (indeed another of MTV's founders, John Lacke, called MTV 'vi-sual radio'), with planned song rotation (Roe & Wallis 1989). However, after some audience decline in the mid 1980s, MTV reduced its dependence on the standard music video clip in favour of more general lifestyle program-ming.

The main purpose of MTV is to deliver a particular audience segment to advertisers. According to one of MTV-Europe's earliest publicity brochures:

Audience research surveys prove that MTV-Europe delivers the audiences advertisers want to reach . . . Nobody reaches the elusive affluent 16–34 audience like
MTV . . . MTV re-writes the rules of European advertising . . . Now advertisers
can hit the 16–34 age group with MTV's laser-sharp targeting . . . MTV reaches
its viewers all over Europe with consistent clarity. It's about the cars they drive,
the clothes they wear, the foods they fuel themselves with, MTV is their choice
(Roe & Wallis 1989).

In order to fulfil this promise to deliver a particular youth market to particular
advertisers, everything on MTV – from the looks and presentation style of
the VJs (video jockeys), the music, and the videos themselves – must fit into
the narrow-casting prescription of what is perceived to appeal to this audience group, namely a non-stop, on-tap, creation of 'moods', 'feelings' and
'emotions' within a youth culture lifestyle that viewers can buy into (Savage
1987, Burnett 1990). In other words, on MTV program content and advertising become to a large extent indistinguishable.

As a result of its success MTV has also had a profound effect on the whole
music recording industry. Suddenly artists and labels felt themselves required to produce sophisticated, expensive music videos in order to promote
their products. Consequently, according to some observers, music video has
not necessarily been an unqualified blessing for the recording industry, especially since there is little firm evidence that music videos actually lead to increased sales of recordings; or that they make any economic sense at all
(Wallis & Malm 1988). Moreover, some artists, are concerned that music
television has resulted in the domination of visual images of 'pretty people'
at the expense of musical talent (Burnett 1996); a domination which, according to some critics, has also led to the re-enforcement of racial and sexual
stereotypes (Brown & Campbell 1986; Kaplan 1987; Seidman 1992).

The MTV audience

Although there is a substantial number of studies of MTV, the great majority
(see e.g. Baxter et al. 1985; Caplan 1985; Aufderheide 1986; Elg & Roe
1986; Sherman & Dominick 1986; Hansen & Hansen 1990; Hansen & Krygowski 1994; Tapper, Thorson & Black 1994; McKee & Pardun 1999) have
dealt with its content and style (usually in terms of its alleged racist, sexist
and 'postmodern' character) rather than with its audience.

In an early study of the American audience Sun & Lull (1986) identified
the importance of the visual aspect of music videos (combined with a gener-
alized attraction to the musical content of MTV) as central to their appeal.
They also found the main motives for viewing to be for entertainment, information, social interaction (talking about videos with friends), and the fact

that videos assisted the interpretation of lyrics. Meanwhile, Brown, Campbell & Fisher (1986: 28) reported that, by that time, 'music videos already had become an important part of the American adolescent's pattern of media use.' In their study the primary motivations for viewing were entertainment, diversion and filling time, social interaction, and to receive instruction on how to dance and what to wear to be fashionable. However, the fact that significant racial and gender differences were found suggested that different adolescent subgroups use videos for different reasons, a conclusion which was supported by Brown & Schulze's (1990) finding that audience interpretations of music videos vary according to race, gender and fandom.

In Europe, the Swedish audience for the music videos on 'Music Box' was studied by Roe & Lövgren (1988). They found that music video TV was already being used on a daily basis by the majority of adolescents in cabled areas. On weekdays, the average time per day spent watching music videos was just under an hour, rising to about 1¼ hours at weekends, although there were some gender differences in this respect. The main motivations for use were found to be passing the time, listening to lyrics, facilitating social activity, and mood control. They also found that school achievement and commitment to school were related to music video use, with low achieving and negative to school adolescents watching significantly more (cf. Roe 1985, 1992, 1993, 1994).

In a study of Flemish adolescents (aged 12–18 years) Roe & Cammaer (1993) found high levels of familiarity with MTV contents. Less than 2% of respondents stated that they knew nothing about MTV, while 73% were able to name at least five MTV programmes. 26% watched the channel on a daily basis, with a further 16% watching at least every other day, and only 10% reported never watching MTV (of these one-third were unable to receive the channel). There was a tendency for frequency of viewing to increase with age, mainly as a result of falling levels of non-viewing. However, most MTV use was found to be unplanned and erratic with viewers 'zapping' in and out of the channel on a regular basis. Further evidence that MTV was regarded as an 'on tap' resource for unplanned viewing was supported by the fact that few ever bothered to use a VCR to record specific MTV programmes. As in other studies, significant gender (and here socio-economic status) differences were found with respect to most aspects of MTV use.

In this Flemish study, the strongest motive for watching MTV was 'to hear the music'. Next came 'relaxation', 'to relieve boredom', 'for information', and 'to be able to talk to others about it', in that order. Attitudes to MTV were generally positive. When asked to rate MTV in terms of seven pairs of positive and negative adjectives, on every dimension the mean fell on the positive side of the scale. MTV was rated most positively in terms of being 'cool', 'novel', 'exciting', and 'amusing'. However, there was less consensus with regard to the musical balance of MTV. Only in one case was there a clear majority opinion: namely, that there was too much rap on MTV. For other music types opinion was more divided and it was concluded that, given the diversity of musical tastes, MTV could do no more than please most of the people some of the time (Roe & Cammaer 1993).

MTV-Europe confronted by linguistic and cultural diversity

Although its growth in terms of household connection figures has been spectacular, MTV-Europe did not enjoy the same immediate financial success as the American parent company and has always suffered from the problem of adapting the channel to the musical, cultural, and linguistic diversity of the continent.

Initially, MTV tackled the problem of satisfying the heterogeneity of music tastes among its audience by putting together varied play lists and strict application of the '5 minute rule', which works on the principle that if the viewer doesn't like what's on at any particular moment, s/he knows that in five minutes time something else will come along. The main problem for MTV-Europe was that, in the vast majority of cases, even this 'something else' tended to be American, leading to accusations that MTV was trying to steamroller Europe with American music and that, in reality, 'globalization' merely meant 'Americanization'. From the beginning MTV-Europe has denied this charge, claiming that it wanted to pay more attention to the European music scene, but that the real problem was the insufficient number of quality European music videos being produced (Roe & Wallis 1989).

Since MTV-Europe is dependent on the international music industry for its program content (i.e. music video clips), it has always been forced to operate within the structural and economic parameters set by that industry, in particular, its Anglo-American dominance. Thus, even when MTV-Europe attempted to reduce its dependence on American music, 'non-American' tended in practice to mean 'British', with the result that in the early years of MTV-Europe, Anglo-American music accounted for 83% of the videos in the total playlist (Burnett 1990).

Given the world-wide popularity of Anglo-American music this in itself does not pose too much of a problem for MTV-Europe. However, it does tend to exacerbate the second cultural problem with which any transnational channel in Europe is inevitably confronted, namely, the continent's linguistic diversity.

Initially, MTV-Europe decided to concentrate on English as its main language because it was perceived to be the most widely spoken, especially among young people. Early experiments with programs in other languages (e.g. Dutch) had merely led to complaints from viewers in other areas. Moreover, language was regarded as of secondary importance compared to the 'universal' language of (Anglo-American) popular music. There is evidence that MTV-Europe's early (American) programmers overestimated the level of comprehension of English among young people on the continent (Roe & Wallis 1989). However, since the program format consisted almost entirely of music videos interspersed by minimal '5 minute rule' links from VJs, language continued to be perceived as unproblematic.

For a time research tended to support this view. For example, even in language-conscious Flanders, the majority of Roe & Cammaer's (1993) 12–18 year old respondents did not perceive language to be a problem on MTV-Europe, with 20% claiming to understand all, and 52% most, of the English spoken on the channel and only 24% stating that they would watch more MTV if there were more programs in Dutch (the language of Flanders).

However, subsequent developments have undermined these assumptions. First, after suffering problems of audience fatigue similar to those earlier experienced by the parent American station, MTV-Europe followed the latter policy of reducing the predominance of the video clip rotation format in favour of other, more talk-based, types of programming. However, this resulted not only in greater demands being made on viewers language comprehension, but to a growing perception that MTV was becoming just another entertainment channel and in danger of losing its special music identity, leading to the cancellation of some non-music programming (Music & Copyright 1997: 123).

Second, and far more seriously, the launch of the German language music television station VIVA in one of MTV-Europe's most important markets brought direct competition for advertising revenue. Viva was set up by four international record companies (PolyGram, EMI, Sony & Warner) in October 1993 and began transmission two months later. By 1997, VIVA was reaching 22 million homes in Germany, Austria and Switzerland, could be received in 96% of German cabled households, and had become more popular than MTV-Europe in its home territories (Music & Copyright 1997: 117). A year later VIVA had further increased its audience in Germany by 26% and was being watched by an estimated 3.9 million viewers a day (6.9% of the German population aged 14-plus), compared to 2.7 million for MTV (Music & Copyright 1998: 142). In the wake of its success a sister channel (VIVA2) was launched early in 1995 to cater for an older age group (as a competitor to MTV's adult music channel VH-1). It too was successful, reaching 63% of all German cabled homes within two years.

VIVA's formula was not only based on having it's VJs speak German rather than English. The management policy of having a quota of German music of 40% for VIVA and 30% for VIVA2 appears to have struck a positive chord with the audience, as well as having stimulated domestic production of records and video clips (Music & Copyright 1997: 117).

It was not long before the success of VIVA called forth imitators in other countries. In the Netherlands, for example, TMF (The Music Factory) was launched in May 1995 and, like VIVA in Germany, it soon displaced MTV-Europe as the most popular music television station in its domestic market (Het Nieuwsblad 12/9/98). The policy of TMF is to feature Dutch VJs who put a lot of emphasis on Dutch musical products and, like VIVA, it works with a 40% quota of domestic video clips. As a result the number of Dutch hits in the national hit parade has risen steadily in the past three years (http://www.tmf.be).

In October 1998, urged on by its success in the Netherlands, TMF established a separate Flemish service (TMF-Vlaanderen) based on the same formula of trying to reflect national tastes and promote local artists and, once again, the formula proved to be successful (Sobemap 1998).

MTV-Europe has admitted that the success of these national imitators (and of VIVA, in particular), forced it to rethink its structure and programming strategy. Its response, in March, 1996, was to create three zones of regionalized programming: (central, northern and southern), followed in July 1997 by a separate UK service.

This 'regional expansion strategy' involved variations in both musical and linguistic content. MTV-UK has a very British character and is dominated by Anglo-American music. MTV-Central is aimed primarily at German-speaking Europe (although it can also be seen in Eastern Europe), with a number of programmes being presented in that language and 20–25% of the video clips featuring local artists. MTV-Southern targeted Italy, where MTV-Europe had always been weak. After its re-launch in September 1997, it contains a substantial number of programs aimed specifically at the Italian market, while 30–35% of the video clips reportedly feature local artists (Bekaert 1998b). Within a few months it had become available to 75% of the Italian population. In France and Spain, however, expansion has proved far more difficult. Levels of cable and satellite penetration remain low in both countries and France has laws specifying language content quotas for television. Consequently, MTV is reportedly more interested in creating local programming for the Netherlands and Scandinavia than increasing its reach in France (Music & Copyright 1997: 123). MTV-Northern is designed to cover the areas not served by the other three and can be received in 25 European and 3 non-European (Egypt, Israel and South Africa) countries. As a result of this diversity it lacks any real regional profile. Its VJs speak English and, despite the fact that recently more Swedish and Dutch artists have been featured (usually singing in English), it remains Anglo-American dominated (Bekaert 1998b).

The results of a content analysis of the programming of MTV-Europe's four regional services, recently undertaken by Keith Roe and Gust De Meyer (Roe and De Meyer 2000), indicate that, while MTV-Central and MTV-Southern have indeed abandoned English as their dominant spoken language, in terms of the origins of the artists and the language of the songs purveyed by

MTV-Europe, nothing appears to have changed since its introduction: 10 years ago 83% of the video clips on MTV-Europe featured British or American artists, today that figure is 82%. Even on MTV-Central and MTV-Southern, German and Italian artists account for only 11% and 17%, respectively, of video clips. Moreover, the fact that 95% of the artists in our study sang in English indicates that some choose that language in preference to their own, presumably in order to increase their chances of receiving international playtime. In terms of its advertising, too, MTV-Europe manifests a very narrow range of products, with five types accounting for over 60% of all advertising spots.

Given these results, we can conclude that it is spoken language (rather than musical tastes) which has proved to be the main obstacle to the success of MTV-Europe. Moreover, despite its regional strategy, own language rivals continue to out-compete MTV-Europe in a number of important markets. Given all of these developments, it is expected that MTV-Europe will be forced to continue its policy of regional differentiation. In particular, it is to be anticipated that the polyglot MTV-Northern service, currently lacking any real profile (and containing the most non-music content), will be carved up into separate sub-segments, with Scandinavia and Dutch-speaking Europe the leading candidates for autonomy. Whether this will result in more Scandinavian and Dutch/Flemish artists singing in their native languages rather than in English, however, remains to be seen.

MTV and globalization

We shall end this paper by attempting to place the experience of MTV-Europe in the context of the discourse surrounding the concept of globalization. In their introduction to a special issue of *Communication Research* dealing with this concept, Riley and Monge (1998: 355) defined globalization as referring, 'to the idea that the world is becoming one place as opposed to a myriad of relatively independent, different and faraway places'.

Proponents of this theory claim that technologies such as communications satellites and the Internet are cutting across local and national cultures and stimulating the creation of a 'global community', while critics point to the manifest tensions which exist in the world between local and global concerns as evidence of its inaccuracy and heuristic frailty. For their part, Riley & Monge (ibid: 356) joined the ranks of the sceptics in concluding that the image of a global community may prove to be illusory, depending on its definitional requirements.

This scepticism has been echoed by many others. For example, Wheeler (1998: 359) claimed that the theory of globalization underestimates the resilience of local identity and cultural differences since local cultural frameworks play an important and under-recognized role in the kinds of practices that are enabled by networked communications. She likened constructing a global culture to, 'putting together a culturally incompatible orchestra', with the inevitable discordant, cacophonous result. Similarly, Waisbord (1998: 377) was unconvinced that current theory fully explains the relations between media and identity – whether at the local, regional, national or global levels – since it conflates media availability and exposure with identity. Consequently:

> It is questionable . . . to conclude that the trans-nationalization of media economies ushers cultural homogenization that paves over differences rooted in local and national cultures (ibid: 385).

In particular, he argues, it is a mistake to equate media availability and exposure – or awareness of distant events, places and cultures – with shared feelings of cultural community or transnational identity. On the contrary, the endurance of local identities in the face of the global media offensive leads Waisbord to conclude that media globalization does not inevitably foster shared supranational cultures and identities and that the relation between the media and cultural identity is more complex than the mediacentric approach, with its strong assumption about the cultural effects of technology, suggests.

What then does 'globalization' actually mean? Giving a direct answer to this question has been complicated by a tendency to conflate the undoubted commodification of the global *economy* with the empirically far more dubious homogenization of global *culture*. This misconception of attributing to things qualities which only human beings could possess is what Marx called the 'fetishism of commodities', a reification which accords these forms of value leading roles in what remains a human drama (Ollman 1971: 198). The fact that global capitalist enterprises seek to promote an *ideology* of cultural homogenization should not, as Wheeler (1998) argued, deceive us into believing that this desire automatically and uniformly results in conformity to a single shared global identity. Thus, we may share Tomlinson's (1999: 85) conclusion that:

> What all this suggests . . . is that arguments which extrapolate from the global ubiquity of capitalist consumer goods and media texts towards the vision of a uniform capitalist monoculture are to be doubted precisely because they trade in a flawed concept of culture.

The question is, rather than talking about *a* flawed concept of culture should we not be talking about *the* flawed concept of culture since, directly or indirectly, what everyone seems to be implying is that we are once again caught up on the familiar merry-go-round of defining it (cf. Riley & Monge above). The marvellous thing about culture, as Cultural Studies has discovered to its own advantage, is that you can make it mean almost anything you want it to mean. Unfortunately, as has often been remarked, with the result that it ends up meaning nothing. Above all it is necessary to avoid flattening out the concept of global culture, of reducing it merely to common patterns of commodity consumption. As Wheeler (ibid: 361) asks sarcastically:

> Does global culture mean the whole world loves McDonald's cheeseburgers and Mickey Mouse? Do the foundations of global community involve everyone in the world watching CNN . . . and in English.

And, we may add, 'watching MTV – and in English?'.

In fact, the case of MTV demonstrates that 'globalization' and 'global culture' are multi-level concepts and suggests that global culture may indeed turn out to involve complexly shifting forms of cultural hybridity (Tomlinson 1999). On one level MTV is a spectacular example of the validity of the globalization thesis: first, it uses contemporary technology to deliver essentially the same product (predominantly Anglo-American music video clips) and the same commodity advertisements (cola, sports shoes, jeans etc.) to the same demographic group all over the world; second, many of the uses and gratifications associated with MTV are in many respects strikingly similar among young people in divergent cultures; and third, MTV has (until now at least) been financially successful in this enterprise. On another level, however, the experience of MTV has been an excellent illustration of the limitations of the globalization idea. Confronted by European cultural and linguistic diversity, MTV has been forced to retreat from its original 'One Planet – One Music' (and 'one language') concept. Moreover, espousing as it does the ideology of globalization, MTV did not compromise willingly with such diversity – it was not until competition from local music television stations began hitting viewing figures (and thereby advertising revenue and profits) that anything but lip-service was paid to the idea of regionalizing European services to cater for local variations.

However, while regionalization has been successful in areas (such as Italy) where the service was previously weak, in areas such as Germany and the Low Countries, where local competition has been effective, MTV-Europe still lags behind in popularity. If the 'universal language of music' has been unable fully to deliver global homogenization, then it is difficult to see how other types of services can hope to succeed except in a very limited superficial sense. Significantly, in September 1997, CNN also adopted a regionalized structure designed to deliver specific services to different parts of the world.

The story of MTV, then, teaches us to be cautious and subtle about the nature of globalization and the forms it may take. *While music television as a format* may be global and here to stay (at least for the foreseeable future), it is by no means certain that *MTV as a channel, at least in its current form,* will be able to maintain its global grasp far into the new century.

Note

*   An earlier version of this article was published in J. Wieten, G. Murdock and P. Dahlgren (eds). *Television Across Europe: A Comparative Introduction*. London: Sage. Reprinted by permission of Sage Publications Ltd.

References

Aufderheide, P. (1986). 'Music Videos; The Look of The Sound.' *Journal of Communication.* 36. 1, 57–78.

Banks, J. (1996). *Monopoly Television: MTV's Ouest To Control The Music.* Boulder, Co: Westview Press.

Baxter, R. L., De Reimer, C., Landini, A., Leslie, L. & Singletary, M. W. (1985). 'A Content Analysis of Music Videos.' *Journal of Broadcasting and Electronic Media.* 29.3, 333–340.

Bekaert, M. (1998a). *Hoe Europees is MTV-Europe?.* Leuven: Departement Communicatie-wetenschap.

Bekaert, M. (1998b). 'De Regionalisering van muziekzenders in Europa.' *Mediagids.* 2, 43–51.

Broadcasting & Cable (1990). *MTV: Moving With The Music.* 2.7. 1990, 39–40.

Brown, J. D. & Campbell, K. (1986). 'Race and Gender in Music Videos: The same Beat but A Different Drummer.' *Journal of Communication.* 36.1, 94–106.

Brown, J. D., Campbell, K. & Fischer, L. (1986). 'American Adolescents and Music Videos: Why Do They Watch?' *Gazette.* 37, 19–32.

Brown, J. D. & Schulze, L. (1990). 'The Effects of Race, Gender, and Fandom on Audience Interpretations of Madonnals Music Videos.' *Journal of communication.* 40.2, 88–102.

Burnett, R. (1990). 'From A Whisper To a Scream: Music Video and Cultural Form.' In: K. Roe & U. Carlsson (eds). *Popular Music Research.* Goeteborg: NORDICOM.

Burnett, R. (1996). *The Global Jukebox.* London: Routledge.

Caplan, R. E. (1985). 'Violent Program Content in Music Video.' *Journalism Quarterly.* 62.1, 144–147.

Denisoff, S. R. (1988). *Inside MTV.* New Brunswick, N. J: Transaction Books.

Elg, P-E & Roe, K. (1986). 'The Music of The Spheres: Satellites and Music Video Content.' - *The NORDICOM Review of Nordic Mass Communication Research.* 2, 15–19.

Hansen, C. H. & Hansen, R. D. (1990). 'The Influence of Sex and Violence On The Appeal of Rock Music Videos.' *Communication Research.* 17.2, 212–234.

Hansen, C. H. & Krygowski, W. (1994). 'Arousal-Augmentation Priming Effects: Rock Music Videos and sex object Schemas.' *Communication Research.* 21.1, 24–47.

Hartman, J. K. (1987). 'I Want My Ad-TV'. *Popular Music and Society.* 11.2, 17–24.

Kaplan, E. A. (1987). *Rocking Around The Clock: Music Television, Postmodernism, & Consumer Culture.* New York: Methuen.

McKee, K.B, & Pardun, C. J. (1999). 'Reading The Video: A Qualitative Study of Religious Images in Music Videos.' *Journal of Broadcasting and Electronic Media.* 43.1, 110–122.

Montavelli, J. (1986). 'MTV sees low cost programming ingenuity as key to sustaining high profitability.' *Cable Vision.* 15. 9. 1986, 26–28.

Ollman, B. (1971). *Alienation: Marx's Conception of Man in Capitalist Society.* Cambridge: University Press.

Pittman, R. W. (1990). 'The Television Generation Speaks A Different Tongue.' *New York Herald Tribune.* 25. 1. 1990, 5.

Riley, P. & Monge, P. R. (1998). 'Communication in The Global Community'. *Communication Research.* 25.4, 355–358.

Roe, K. (1985). 'The School and Music In Adolescent Socialization.' In: J. Lull (ed). *Popular Music and Communication.* Newbury Park, Ca: Sage.

Roe, K. (1992). 'Different Destinies – Different Melodies: School Achievement, Anticipated Status and Adolescents' Tastes In Music.' *European Journal of Communication.* 7.3, 335–357.

Roe, K. (1993). 'Academic Capital and Music Tastes Among Swedish Adolescents: An Empirical Test of Bourdieu's Model of Cultural Reproduction.' *Young: The Nordic Journal of Youth Research.* 1.3, 40–55.

Roe, K. (1994). 'Media Use and Social Mobility'. In: K. E. Rosengren (ed). *Media Effects and Beyond.* London: Routledge.

Roe, K & Cammaer, G. (1993). 'Delivering The Young Audience To Advertisers.' *Communications: The European Journal of Communication.* 18.2, 169–177.

Roe, K. & De Meyer, G. (2000). 'MTV-Europe: One Music – Many Languages?' In: J. Wieten, G. Murdock and P. Dahlgren (eds). Television Across Europe: A Comparative Introduction. London: Sage

Roe, K. & Loevgren, M. (1988). 'Music Video and Educational Achievement'. *Popular Music.* 7.3, 303–313.

Roe, K. & Wallis, R. (1989). 'One Planet One Music': The Development of Music Television in Western Europe.' *The NORDICOM Review of Nordic Mass Communication Research.* 1989/1, 34–39.

Savage, J. (1987). 'Latched Onto The Loop'. *The Observer.* 16. 8. 1997.

Seidman, S. (1992). 'An Investigation of Sex-Role Stereotyping in Music Videos.' *Journal of Broadcasting and Electronic Media.* 36.2, 209–216.

Sherman, B. L. & Dominick, J. R. (1986). 'Violence and Sex In Music Videos.' *Journal of Communication.* 36.1, 79–93.

Straw, W. (1988). 'Music Video in its Contexts: Popular Music and Post-Modernism in the 1980's'. *Popular Music.* 7.3, 247–266.

Sun, S.-W. & Lull, J. (1986). 'The Adolescent Audience For Music Videos and Why They Watch.' *Journal of Communication.* 36.1, 115–125.

Tapper, J., Thorson, E. & Black, D. (1994). 'Variations in Music Videos As A Function of Their Musical Genre.' *Journal of Broadcasting and Electronic Media.* 38.1, 103–113.

Tomlinson, J. (1999). *Globalization and Culture.* Cambridge: Polity Press.

Waisbord, (1998). 'When The Cart of Media is Put Before The Horse of Identity.' *Communication Research.* 25.4, 377–398.

Wheeler, D. K. (1998). 'Global Culture or Global Clash'. *Communication Research.* 25.4, 359–376.

Part II:
Beyond the transnational music industry – The global use and abuse of popular music

4 Sampling the didjeridoo

Susanne Binas

The various forms of popular music are the results of profound technological and social modernization processes starting from North America and Europe which have cultural constellations worldwide. At the end of this century popular music is characterized by the tension of local musical practices in between global cultural processes.

Just at the time when local music traditions had first been fixed on records, when record companies founded subsidiaries in faraway countries to expand their markets, or when musicians from former countries of the colonial empire were playing in dance-halls of European cities, popular music became a transcultural phenomenon.

Now as everywhere discussion of social, economic and cultural globalization has begun, also those musical forms – which have become noticeable by their transcultural characteristics – have received increasing attention. Styles like world music, tribal dance or sample beats consisting of indigenous sound patterns seem to be a suitable area for investigations which deal with musical globalization or localization. They refer to currents of sounds and symbols which regardless of the real distances between popular music production and the locations of their traditional use will become universally available.

Sounds are traveling around the world on acoustic databases or with globally organized record companies. Within these processes cultural-aesthetic and economic areas of contradiction and conflicts have arisen which can not really be depicted in polarized terms as 'local' and 'global', 'real' and 'media' or 'authentic' and 'commercial'.

But how could these processes be described adequately? Why are certain sounds or rhythms of such great interest to some practitioners? Why and how did they come, e.g. from West Africa to London, from the Mongolian steppe to European concert halls, or from the Australian bush to the chill-out rooms of techno parties in cities? And in the reverse case in which way did the cultural standards of 'Western' pop music enter into the former? All of them are now part of a global cultural economy and circulate in transnational networks of practice, commodities and aesthetics.

There are always various participants with different interests in the music process who are responsible for the exchange of cultural features. At first there were the slaves, and later ethnologists; during the first years of the 20th century, in particular, there were recording teams from the still-young record companies, the traveling musicians searching for new aesthetic material, and we are now facing sound engineers, event agencies, tourists and civilization-diseased city dwellers longing for exotic music. Already this disordered enumeration let us foresee what kind of complicated area of historically concrete investigation we are now confronted with.

How could it be possible to understand the complexity to reconstruct or 'measure' relations of effects? Already the empirical database given by the phonographic industries is not as real an empirical basis, as scholars often emphasize (see especially Harker 1997 or Wicke 1997a).

To make it more difficult most of the debates on cultural globalization and localization are not free of moralizing and sweeping statements and judgements about it. Between the places of the globally linked world obviously an immense power difference of economics still exists and we have to be aware of that.

From the perspective of studies in musicology we are confronted with an additional problem. Even when methods of social science are used, most of the investigations are based on an understanding of music which conceptualizes it as something which, properly measured, apparently could expose hidden sections pars pro toto. But popular music is – Peter Wicke (1995) wrote – 'a result of complex musical, cultural and commercial activities which are absolutely full of inconsistencies, always socially structured, and bounded on the media of sound. These activities will be realized through and within this media but they do not simply leave a copy, which could be decoded like an impression'.

Because of that I want to try to reconstruct a concrete example – the emergence of one of the oldest instruments of the world, the didjeridoo with its specific sound as a tool for articulating cultural meaning and/or memory.

Depending on the space available here I'll only want to have a look at the technological dimension of this process, exchange and appropriation to reconstruct some of the relevant relations of effects.

The didjeridoo between aboriginal traditions and the 'universal pop aesthetic'

The approach

When I started my research of local music cultures within the global process in the mid 1990s it was less the theoretical paradigms of homogenization and differentiation, Americanization or transculturation that attracted my attention than certain cultural-aesthetic phenomena: sold-out drum workshops, 'Salsatheques', or didjeridoos in the chill-out rooms of techno parties in Berlin. As a former active musician I was especially interested in the variety and the availability of sound patterns which, at first glance, stood in contradiction to the Western image and appreciation of time and space and listening habits.

Appropriation of these musical forms is characterized by enormous rifts in time and space, especially when they take place in urban centres. Sounds and signs, as well as locations, places, history and traditions, become universally available and linked. However, they serve less as a call for traditional contexts, which is my argument, but they are able to construct or replace destabilized cultural identities by projecting one's own desires onto 'other' cultural forms. Categories like 'das Eigene' and 'das Fremde' are quite intertwined. The German philosopher Wolfgang Welsch (1992: 11) wrote: 'Es gibt nicht nur kein strikt Fremdes, sondern auch kein strikt Eigenes mehr. Authentizität ist zum Bestandteil der Folklore geworden, ist simulierte Eigenheit für andere, zu denen man als Einheimischer längst selbst gehört.'

Last but not least 'World Music' as a commercial category was 'found' in 1987 for those socially structured cultural needs and musical phenomena which were clearly marked by musical crossover, transculturation and non-Western traditions. 'One of the obstacles in persuading record shops to stock much of the new international products was reported to be the lack of an identifying category to describe it' (see especially Taylor 1997), and this category also was created as a marketing strategy to speak to those people who didn't confront themselves with the pressure of rationalization and civilization by Western societies (students, alternative life-stylists, etc.). In their search for 'authenticity' and 'originality' they really and virtually went into those regions of the world which don't seem to be affected by technology and the processes of commodification. But especially those phenomena – like the development of phonographic technologies, the music industry, event-culture or 'festivalization' of the culture – became important opportunities to feed the longings for 'the other shore' to satisfy cultural needs without the necessity for real (expensive) traveling.

The didjeridoo within a multiple scenario of cultural uses

The 'modernization' of the didjeridoo, one of the oldest instruments in the world, is probably the most conspicuous phenomena of its kind. This transformation serves as a suitable example for examining those processes which have been discussed and analyzed under the heading of 'cultural globalization' for a considerable time. My preliminary investigations showed that the instrument and its sound have emerged in a series of very different cultural-aesthetic contexts. Concentrating on the 1980s and 1990s, I found the didjeridoo in the contexts of New Age, World Music, Rock, Pop, Jazz and New Music. I would like to point out that my study of the didjeridoo was not so much a quantitative survey as a qualitative analysis of specific cases.

The emergence of the didjeridoo is not evident in statistics of the music industry. Nevertheless, it is a useful example to trace the peculiar paths and problems of cultural globalization.

Every person – whether a musician, performer, journalist, promoter, listener or alternative therapist, to give some examples – has a different motivation for their interest in the didjeridoo. The result is a multiple scenario of cultural use.

The examples I'll briefly discuss here probably could be considered representative though I don't claim that they are complete:

Example 1: The traditional context Songs from the Northern Territory (Institute for Traditional Music – Berlin/University of Bamberg)

Before I discuss the examples I should briefly give a general idea of the didjeridoo within its traditional context of use.

Traditional aboriginal music is primarily a vocal art form rather than an instrumental one. The so-called song lines apply to the mythology of a specific clan, also they give practical instructions for the cultivation of the countryside, toxic fruits and animals and they provide information about the topography of landscapes.

Each verse consists of a limited number of words with many different meanings. The rhythmic relationships between the words and accompanying musical instruments are constantly shifted and varied. Percussion (idiophones such as clapsticks, rasps and seed rattles) and the didjeridoo (an aerophone – sound is produced by means of vibrating air) also provides accompaniment to both song and dance, and aboriginal musical instruments are essentially rhythmic in purpose (Neuenfeldt 1993: 62).

As the song lines tell stories about the ancestors and the landscape, they also imitate the behavior or motions of animals, their sounds, the jumping of a frog or the flapping of birds' wings in narrative structures as an important part of the aboriginal dreamtime mythology.

The term 'didjeridoo' itself is of unknown origin. Some scholars suggest that '. . . although now commonly called by this name, which is probably of European onomatopoeic intent, some 40 aboriginal names for it are used in the various northern regions where it is traditional used, while others suggest that the non-aboriginal term "didjeridoo" has been derived quite recently from sounds made by this lip-buzzed aerophone' (Moyle 1981: 321).

Example 2: A didjeridoo at a techno party 'Lucifer's Techno Dada' (Sydney Rave) with Louis Burdett, Janawirri Yiparrka & DJ Zeitgeist (recorded at E-Werk, Berlin, on April 3 1995)

Lets start with an event which took place at a well-known techno location (E-Werk) in Berlin in 1995. You will not really hear the didjeridoo because of the difficult acoustics and the balance between the various sound sections mixed by the DJs and the didjeridoo which was played by Janawirri Yiparrka.

Probably this was quite an experiment (subsonic frequencies) announced as part of a major rave party, conceived and orchestrated by Louis Burdett, featuring Kirilly Smitheran alias DJ Zeitgeist from Sydney (member of Clan Analogue, a collective for electronic arts), Janawirri Yiparrka (born in 1967, descended from the Wongi and Ngaanjatjarra peoples of the Western Desert in West Australia, took up the didjeridoo at the age of nine, has performed publicly at both Aborigine and urban cultural venues since 1988, appearances in various contexts, at exhibitions and festivals on art and music of the Aborigines, festivals and concerts of world music, shows such as 'Der große Preis' [ZDF TV network] and Oktoberfest, dance parties, European tour with the Australian band Wizards of Oz) and many others.

Example 3: Circular breathing from the CD 'living structures' by Circular Breathing (Janusphere 10194-1)

The band Circular Breathing – consisting of three European musicians living in Berlin – would describe their project as a part of the World Music and Ethno-Jazz context. All of them are passionate didjeridoo players who sometimes visit Australia. However, they don't understand their music as an attempt to reproduce traditional aboriginal music. They own a lot of didjeridoos which can be used in different variations on stage and in the studio to produce their songs.

During an interview I conducted with them the leader of the band, who is also the owner of a small independent label and a distribution company for didjeridoos, emphasized that he is especially interested in the sound material and techniques of playing opposed to the obligation of the artificial European traditions like the reading of music or attending music schools. He likes the didjeridoo as an instrument which offers the occasion to create lively musical structures. An unprejudiced listener would hear complex sections of standards and improvised parts mixing various instruments, sounds and rhythms from 'non-Western' music – like the tabla. But the band knows that if they want to sell their CDs successfully they have to promote them within the context and categories of New Age and esoteric distribution. The booklet contains the following sentences:

CIRCULAR BREATHING, as our band name, stands for the analogy between our music, using the ever repeating yet slightly changing rhythmic and harmonic structures, and the circular changes of nature. Breathing – the essence of life, filling the didjeridoo with sound, connects the inner and the outer world. By synchronizing our breathing, we, the three parts of the circle, with our different styles of playing, form a higher unity. The contrast between the deep droning tone and the inherent overtones, express the perceived polarity between the absolute reality and the relative world, which is known to all mystical traditions. The sound thus reminds us of the essential unity of these two poles.

On this occasion I am unable to pursue the question of how the didjeridoo is used in New Age contexts, therapy and healing arts. Nevertheless I know that this is a main area where it is used outside its traditional context (see especially Stroh 1994 or Neuenfeldt 1998).

Example 4: Yothu Yindi's TREATY Radio Mix (1992 Mushroom Records TVD 91017)

There is one Australian band which could fill pages or books discussing their development. Especially in Australia where a detailed debate took place on the effects of mixing 'authentic' aboriginal sounds, images and the standards of rock and pop music as Yothu Yindi does constantly. The sounds and visions are focused on traditional instruments, especially the didjeridoo and the birma.

Rather than pursue this topic now, I would like to turn our attention directly towards the dimension of technologizing old instruments like the didjeridoo.

From the perspective of technology and material culture the traditional Australian didjeridoo could serve as a prime example of 'low-tech' (see Neuenfeld 1993). Karl Neuenfeldt has done a lot of research relating to this band and the subject of the didjeridoo. In his article 'The Didjeridoo and the Overdub – Technologising and Transposing Aural Images of Aboriginality' (1993) he wrote 'especially while recording the hit song "TREATY" and the album *Tribal Voice* the record producer (Mark Moffit) and the band responded innovatively to the challenges of melding traditional elements in their music with the standard rock and roll rhythm section of bass, drums, guitar and keyboard'. The record producer commented on how the didjeridoo was recorded in order to blend it with the rhythm section's backing tracks for the non-traditional songs on the album:

> Technically (what we did) was figure out a way to play along with each yidaki (didjeridoo) on a guitar string and tune the guitar to it . . . and then look at that note on the tuner and put that note on the tape machine at concert pitch and then tune (the tape machine) down to where that note read cuz there's no other way of doing it. And that helped a lot because when it's not it's a terrible sound (Mark Moffit, pop music producer and recording engineer quoted in Neuenfeldt 1993: 65).

Example 5: Jamiroquai's When You Gonna Learn from the CD 'Emergency On Planet Earth' (1993 Sony Soho Square 474069 2) and the *Supersonic Radio Edit* (1999 Sony Soho Square 667777 2)

The acid jazz band Jamiroquai started the first title of their CD 'Emergency On Planet Earth' with an introduction of a didjeridoo solo. This is motivated by the content as well as aesthetically. The whole CD is focused on sources of danger arising from the civilization process, and especially the lyrics and the booklet should us make aware of the archaic and colourful beauty of fantastic untouched nature.

But we have to read it also as a part of a special pop discourse not as a piece of art. The break between the introduction and the song is quite noticeable as well as the didjeridoo part in the middle of the song probably because of the technological problems I quoted in the above-mentioned example.

There are technological problems and aesthetic intentions. In my opinion these didjeridoo parts are used as something like an eye- or 'earcatcher' as is done in advertisements, a label or a sign to aid recognition of this album and concept. This is quite a common practice for differentiating pop songs and also important for the live presentation to be a little bit different from the others.

The recently published song 'Supersonic' – various mixes of which exist – also contains the didjeridoo as one noticeable sound plateau. Now it is much more embedded into the whole sound and has atmospheric features other than qualities of an eyecatcher. The two other mixes which have been produced and published do not contain the sound of the didjeridoo.

Example 6: NIOWT's Horizon (M. Krevel) from the promotion CD (1998 Edition Gym/AMV/Chrom Records/EfA)

The last example was published and edited in 1998 on a promotion sampler of EfA. The sampler collects various songs and tracks between Dub, Drum & Bass, Electro-dance and TripHop.

In all probability the didjeridoo sound which introduces the track is a digital sample that can be used and tuned electronically. Productions, producers or musicians like these are especially interested in particular aesthetic material. Whether from the sampler, sampling CDs or any other sources, it is often used not to quote or refer to anything, but to satiate their thirst for wider sources of material, and it enables a certain behavior of expression. They rarely ask where this sample came from, or whether the sounds link with any particular musical tradition, historical facts or economic injustice.

This example seems to be comparable to recordings we know since a group of DJs in the early 1980s produced a massive hit entitled 'Pump Up the Volume' (M/A/R/R/S).

The song employed more than thirty samples, set over a steady disco rhythm, interspersed with a vocal refrain. Toward the end of the song, a passage of synthetically altered Arab singing is heard over the steady beat, matching the tonality and rhythm of the song. This Arabic singing is clearly not meant to evoke images of

Arabia, . . . the aesthetic here is quintessentially postmodern, involving neither embodied nor referential meaning, but instead revelling in a certain sort of meaninglessness (Manuel 1995: 232).

The development of technology as one driving force of cultural globalization

In each case there is a specific network of relationships in which the traditional meaning of the instrument or of its sound, its origin and/or its ritual contexts are vaguely associated but ultimately dissolved. The patterns of interpretation and the ways in which the instrument and its sound are being used produce new contexts and discourses which give new meanings to signs. One driving force behind these processes of disintegration is the development of phonographic technology.

In conclusion, let me summarize the issues in a more general form. Acoustic phenomena and events have been torn from their original contexts ever since the invention of phonographic equipment, thereby enabling this process. In the first instance this means no more than the detachment of an acoustic phenomenon from its source; 'a voice without a face' as Dave Laing (1991) titled his article about the early time of phonographic technologies. Nowadays we find it completely natural that we perceive and register sounds without seeing those who actually produce the sounds. However, the separation between the 'here' and 'now', the separation between body, motion and sound, has had considerable consequences. Musical-cultural relations were changed drastically with the development of phonographic equipment. Whether traditional music cultures from rural contexts all over the world or the various forms of popular music and also the artificial traditions of Western music, they have all lost their exclusiveness and have become commonly available. Everything that can be stored in digital form can be reproduced, changed, transported over long distances and or re-worked over and over at will.

This development does not only provoke losses but also interesting opportunities as we saw.

Krister Malm (1993: 347/348) indicates that 'the movement of musical sound in time and space is a kind of transplantation of music. The transplantation processes become more and more visible as the years pass. . . . [D]issemination on recorded media has also given music traditions another kind of chance to survive and develop.'

Mankuma Yunupingu, Yothu Yindi's didjeridoo player emphasized that:

. . . these days we're doing more compromising in terms of cultural situations, and you've got to do it because you're dealing with the commercial aspects of the industry. As long as our values, beliefs and principles remain intact then I think that's the way to go – and I think we've got the strength to do that. . . . We don't want to be a museum piece. We aim to make people aware that we have unique culture that can co-exist with Western culture (Hitching 1993; Mitchell 1993: 332).

'Without technology,' as Steve Jones has noted,

popular music would not exist in its present form. Without electronics, and without accompanying technical supports and technical experimentation, there could not be the mass production of music, and therefore there would not be the mass-mediated popular music. Of equal importance, without technology there could not be the creation of sounds that are today intimately associated with popular music. . . . In turn, production and consumption of recordings are profoundly technological (Jones 1990: 1).

At the same time, the universal commodity production reached for the musical cultures of the world. In the search for markets for the hardware (phonographic equipment), the software (various music cultures and their traditions) falls into the system of commercialization, rationalization, the setting-up of corresponding economic organizations (labels, agencies, radio and TV stations, distributors) and the emerging legal systems for the administration of the new property relationships, including copyright issues.

As I tried to describe it with the example of the Australian band Yothu Yindi, undoubtedly it is quite difficult to integrate the didjeridoo within the sound plateau of the international pop aesthetics. But since it has become possible to digitalize its sound the problems of tuning and the spectrum of overtones can be solved. There are really no limits to its use in an electronic studio.

By the way it was Peter Gabriel who took the first didjeridoo samples into the sound-bank of his Real World Studio in the early 1980s.

Digital sounds or binary ones are highly dissected sounds – technically speaking; they consist of 0s and 1s. A bit is the smallest unit of a sign, an elementary or universal sign. At this point the dismantling is finished and the sample has been converted into synthetic power.

Conclusion

The various forms of popular music existing at the turn of the century are results of these profound technological and social modernization processes. The technologies of recording and distribution greatly influence the procedure and rules of how music is made and conceptualized, how music-making can be learned or taught, and how music can be listened to.

The sampler as instrument or the sampling procedure as cultural technique represent these developments in a paradigmatic way. The notions of law and injustice, authorship, creativity and responsibility for cultural traditions and resources – as they were stirred up by this instrument since the mid 1980s at least – concern the whole musical process at a time of continuous globalization.

Therefore I'm convinced that investigating the reconstruction of phonographic developments, the use of instruments, and hard- and software and their effects on the music process could and should be useful for analyzing the relationships between music and globalization.

References

Harker, Dave (1997). 'The wonderful world of IFPI: music industry rhetoric, the critics and the classical marxist critique.' *Popular Music* Volume 16/1, 45–70.

Jones, Steve (1990). 'Technology and the Future of Popular Music.' *Popular Music and Society* Volume 14, No. 1.

Laing, Dave (1991). 'A voice without a face. Popular music and the phonograph in the 1980s.' *Popular Music*. Volume 10, No. 1, January 1991, 1–10.

Malm, Krister (1993). 'Music on the Move: Traditions and Mass Media.' *Ethnomusicology* Volume 37, No. 3, 339–352.

Manuel, Peter (1995). 'Music as symbol, music as simulacrum: postmodern, pre-modern, and modern aesthetics in subcultural popular musics.' *Popular Music* Volume 14, No. 2, 227–239.

Mitchell, Tony (1993). 'World Music and the Popular Music Industry: An Australian View.' *Ethnomusicology* Volume 37, No. 3.

Moyle, A. M. (1981). 'The Australian Didjeridoo: A Late Musical Intrusion.' *World Archaeology* 12.

Neuenfeldt, Karl (1993). 'The Didjeridu and the Overdub. Technologising and Transposing Aural Images of Aboriginality.' *Perfect Beat* Volume 1, No. 2, 60–77.

Neuenfeldt, Karl (1998). 'Good Vibrations? The 'Curious' Cases of the Didjeridu in Spectacle & Therapy in Australia.' *the world of music* Volume 40 (2), 29–51.

Stroh, Wolfgang Martin (1994). 'Die transkulturelle Dimension der New Age Musik.' In: Wolfgang Martin Stroh. *Handbuch New Age Musik. Auf der Suche nach neuen musikalischen Erfahrungen*. Regensburg: ConBrio Verlagsgesellschaft, 311–336.

Taylor, Timothy D. (1997). 'Popular Musics and Globalization – Welcome to the Market.' In: Timothy D. Taylor. *Global Pop. World Music, World Markets*. New York & London: Routledge, 1–21.

Welsch, Wolfgang (1992). 'Transkulturalität. Lebensformen nach der Auflösung der Kulturen.' *Information Philosophie* 1, 5–20.

Wicke, Peter (1995). 'Popmusik – Konsumfetischismus oder kulturelles Widerstandspotential? Gesellschaftliche Dimensionen eines Mythos.' In: Heuger, Marcus & Prell, M. (ed.). *Popmusic yesterday today tomorrow*. Regensburg: ConBrio Verlagsgesellschaft, 21–35.

Wicke, Peter (1997a). 'Popmusik als Industrieprodukt.' http://www2.rz.hu-berlin./de/inside/fpm/musikind.

Wicke, Peter (1997b). 'Die Charts im Musikgeschäft.' http://www2.rz.hu-berlin./de/inside/fpm/musikind.

5 Race, ethnicity and the production of Latin/o popular music

Deborah Pacini Hernandez

Most of the discussion encountered in the US about globalization and popular music has been concerned with the circulation and impact of two major categories of music. One of these is western rock/pop – e.g. musicians such as Madonna, Michael Jackson, or U2, whose records have sold millions of copies all over the globe, but whose influence, in terms of fashion, dance and other patterns of cultural behavior, has extended far beyond the economic transactions involved in record sales. The other category of music commonly referred to in discussions of globalization has been the world music/world beat phenomenon, in which 'non-Western' musics have been circulating widely among multiple global locations, although primarily and most lucratively within the US and Europe; here the concern has largely been with the inequalities between the musicians producing the music, most of whom come from underdeveloped countries, and those who profit by them, most of whom are from wealthy developed countries.[1] There is, however, another major geographic and aesthetic zone of production whose particular position within the increased global circulation of popular musics has received less attention, and which is the subject of this essay: the category referred to as Latin music. In this essay I am going to explore two aspects of Latin music: the first concerns the 'fit' between the category of 'Latin music' and the social groups, which include both Latin Americans and US Latinos, assumed to be producing and consuming it. The second part of this essay explores the impact of transnational migration – a key but often under-appreciated aspect of globalization – on Latino popular musics in the United States.

The politics of commercial labels and ethnic identities

Before one can even begin to discuss the impact of globalization on Latin music, it is necessary to unpack this very flawed and problematic term, which is fraught with unfounded cultural assumptions that generally go unexamined. In order to do this, I need to clarify the important differences between three related but not synonymous terms: 'Latin,' 'Latino,' and 'Latin

American.' 'Latin Americans' refers quite simply to the peoples (and cultures) of the various Latin American nations. In Spanish, Latin Americans – *Latino Americanos* – are sometimes referred to as *Latinos*, as a shorthand term. In the United States, however, the term 'Latino' refers specifically to people with some degree of Latin American ancestry, but whose most important distinction is that they reside permanently in the US. Like the term 'Hispanic' (with which it is often used interchangeably), 'Latino' is a pan-ethnic, pan-national term whose purpose is precisely to differentiate residents of the US who are of Latin American descent from other non-white US minorities – blacks, Asians, etc. – as well as from Latin American nationals.

The terms 'Latino' and 'Hispanic' have generated considerable controversy in the US. The term 'Hispanic' has been criticized for being a term invented and imposed by US officialdom, as well as for privileging connections to peninsular Spain while obscuring the region's predominantly African and Indian demographic and cultural roots. The term 'Latino,' on the other hand, is used by those who prefer it because it connects US Latinos to Latin America rather than to Spain, and because it is perceived as a self-designated rather than an imposed term.

Nevertheless, even the more politically self-conscious term 'Latino' has been criticized by Latinos themselves for effacing the historical and cultural specificities of the many ethnic/racial and national communities that fall under this catch-all rubric (cf. Garcia 2000, Oboler 1995), obscuring the fact that Latinos are, in racial, ethnic, national, class and cultural terms, extremely diverse. For example, it makes no distinctions between Mexicans and Puerto Ricans who were involuntarily absorbed into the US by conquest in the 19th and early 20th century and those who voluntarily migrated to the US; nor does it distinguish between individuals who have lived in the US for generations, many of whom no longer speak Spanish, and recent arrivals who still consider themselves citizens of their home countries; nor does it distinguish between those who are full citizens, legal residents, or undocumented immigrants.

As a result, the term 'Latino' is rejected by those who insist on retaining their specific national identities – they still call themselves Mexicans or Cubans. Nevertheless, I would argue that there is some logic to employing the term selectively, because even while most Latinos maintain some connections – whether physical or emotional – with their various Latin American homelands, all of them have been transformed to some degree by their interactions with the host US culture, in which they are positioned as a racial and cultural minority. As individuals and scholars, we should respect a person's choice of self-identification, but we must also acknowledge differences when they are functionally and analytically significant.

As for the term 'Latin,' it has been around a long time to refer generically to people of Latin American descent, regardless of nationality or citizenship

– as in the term Latin lover (which, I might note, has often included Italians and Spaniards as well). In the 1940s and 50s 'Latin music' was all the rage in the US. The fact that most 'Latin music' was Cuban was unimportant to most North Americans, who did not bother with such distinctions. Nowadays, most English speakers in the US tend not to use the term 'Latin' when referring to people, since they know there is a difference between Latinos and Latin Americans, but the term 'Latin music' continues to be used as a catchall phrase intended to describe all popular music performed and consumed by Latinos and Latin Americans alike. As we shall see, this umbrella term is full of holes.

Using the groundbreaking and insightful work of Keith Negus (1999) on the Latin music industry and its incorporation into the major international music companies as a point of departure, I want to focus here on the reluctance of the music industry to recognize the cultural differences between these groups, as it continues to lump Latino and Latin American music together as if they were one and the same. As used by the industry, the category of Latin music includes a diverse range of styles, from genres such as *merengue*, *tango*, *samba* and *mariachi* which are identified as the 'national' musics of the Dominican Republic, Argentina, Brazil and Mexico, respectively; to newer styles developed by Latinos within the US, such as New York *salsa* and Texas *tejano*; to international styles not connected to any particular place of origin such as *salsa romántica*, *balada*, and the category known as Latin pop. While these musics have little if anything in common aesthetically, they are all mass-mediated urban musics – traditional Peruvian pan pipe music, for example, is not likely to be referred to as Latin music. Significantly, what the term Latin music has not included, at least until recently, is mass mediated urban musics made and consumed by people of Latin American origin when it has been in the rock idiom, whether it is sung in English, Spanish or Spanglish. I will discuss this in more detail below.

Regardless of what one might think about the imprecision and the cultural assumptions behind the category and term Latin music, they cannot be dismissed, because they have been adopted and operationalized by all the major international record companies, which since the 1980s have created Latin divisions, most of them based in the US, created expressly to promote 'Latin' music domestically (within the US), as well as regionally (throughout the hemisphere) and globally – to Europe, Asia and Africa. This imprecise, catch-all term has been complicated and perpetuated by the fact that, as I mentioned above, the Spanish shorthand term for Latin Americans is *Latinos*; therefore, the Spanish term, *música latina*, correctly refers to the music of Latin America. While some might say that this conflation of Latinos and Latin Americans is appropriate within the new global environment in which culture is transnational, and national borders are irrelevant to the flows of cultural products such as music (as well as to flows of the people who produce and consume these musics), the logic behind the creation and maintenance of the Latin music category, as I will discuss further below, is not so benign.

While the term 'Latin music industry' suggests a monolithic entity, this is not the case, as the international music companies are not the only ones producing and promoting Latin music. Competing – and sometimes collaborating – with the majors are vigorous national recording industries in the various Latin American countries, which specialize in locally-produced music for their own domestic markets – although they may market particular artists with 'crossover' potential internationally as well. Additionally, within the US, numerous small, regionally-based independent labels have existed for decades, most of which are Latino-owned, and which cater to ethnically-specific communities, particularly in states with large Latino populations such as California, Texas, New York and Florida. These ethnic labels might also market to the specific 'home' country of the particular ethnic group: for example, *tejano* (i.e. Texas-Mexican) record companies also market their products in Mexico, while New York-based Dominican companies such as J & N also operate in the Dominican Republic. While most Latino-oriented labels in the US are relatively small operations, the international profiles of larger ethnic labels such as RMM can be substantial. These ethnically-oriented record companies, whether large or small, refer to their musics in genre-specific ways – i. e. as tejano, salsa, merengue or *cumbia* – rather than as 'Latin music.' When these same musics are distributed by the majors, however, they are likely to be lumped in with other Latin American music and marketed as Latin.

Together, these companies constitute what we think of as the Latin music industry, and its profitability has been growing by leaps and bounds. The Latin music market is still much smaller than the mainstream US market, but it has expanded dramatically in the wake of the tremendous increases in immigration from Latin America to the US. Now more than 31 million strong, US Latinos constitute over 11% of the US population and within a decade, they will surpass African Americans as the country's largest minority group. Sales of Latin music (and related video products) have doubled in recent years, from $ 260 million in 1995 to $ 570.8 million in 1998, and approximately one third of these profits are generated in the US. This represents only about 5% of total music industry earnings – although its rate of growth has been increasing exponentially: once estimated to grow at between 22% and 24% a year (RIAA 1999), since the Ricky Martin phenomenon, US sales of Latin music have jumped a whopping 54% over the same period 1998 (Taraska 1999). Such figures tend to be conservative, because a lot of Latin music is sold in mom-and-pop stores whose sales are not tallied by Soundscan (Negus 1999). Sales made by small ethnic labels are not likely to figure into these tallies either. Furthermore, a large proportion of Latin recordings sold –

particularly those produced by the majors – are pirated; some have estimated that such 'lost' receipts account for almost half the market.

In spite of these impressive statistics, both the category and term Latin music need to be interrogated. In his 1999 essay, 'The Latin music industry, the production of salsa and the cultural matrix,' Keith Negus deconstructed the Latin music category, showing how the Latin music industry has suffered from the contradictions of being at once a domestic US industry, producing and marketing a variety of regional styles by and for US Latinos, and at the same time, an industry with deep and important connections to Latin America. More problematic, as Negus notes, is that the industry has adopted certain assumptions about Latinos' essential foreignness to domestic American culture, consigning US Latino musicians and styles, along with their Latin American counterparts, to the international divisions.

While on the surface the organizational strategy of combining US Latino and Latin American musics into one division seems to make both cultural and economic sense, the implications of this decision have a profound impact on US Latino artists. First, as Negus points out, they receive less promotional and distributional support than that given to other domestic musics. Furthermore, the personnel in charge of promotion and distribution often do not know about and therefore cannot distinguish between the specificities of the Latin American and US Latino markets. But the consequences of the conflation of Latinos and Latin Americans can be even more insidious: for example, when the majors (Sony, Capitol EMI, WEA, Polygram, Universal and BMG) established their Latin music divisions, all but BMG US Latin and Polygram Latino were set up as independent entities that were not bound by the parent companies' union contracts and the labor practices outlined in the industry-wide Phonograph Record Label Agreement (Burr 1999). This meant that a tejano musician recording for Sony and EMI did not receive the same union scale wages and protections, as say, a musician who recorded country music, or even other 'American' niche musics such as Christian music. Recent statements by an executive with EMI Latino confirm Negus's observations about industry perceptions of US Latinos as being foreign to the cultural fabric of the United States: 'the Latin music business, specifically tejano music, is significantly different – certainly in the way we do it – from the way that traditional, for lack of a better term, anglo business is done' (Patterson 1999).

In addition to ignoring differences between Latin American and US Latino musics, the catch-all Latin music category has also allowed the industry to treat all US Latino musics as an undifferentiated group, obscuring and ignoring the profound differences among the many styles falling under that umbrella term, as well as among the communities that produce and consume them. For readers unfamiliar with the cultural geography of US Latinos, here is a broad summary: in the northeast (especially New York), the Latino population is primarily of Spanish Caribbean origins – Puerto Ricans, Dominicans and Cubans – so Latin music in this region generally refers to Spanish Caribbean musics such as *salsa*, *merengue* and *bachata*, although newer immigrant communities such as Salvadoreans and Colombians have diversified New York's Latin music landscape with musics such as *cumbias* and *vallenatos*. Younger East Coast Latinos from all backgrounds, but especially the US-born, are also making and listening to rap, both African-American and Latino, as well as to house music.

In Texas, the Southwest, and California, in contrast, most Latinos are of Mexican descent, and their musical preferences and practices are very different from those of Spanish Caribbeans. In Texas, the Latino popular music landscape is dominated by accordion-based *conjunto* music, a genre firmly rooted in rural Mexican American communities, and the slicker, urban sounds of tejano – the deceased singer Selena being the most famous example – whose influences include rock, country and pop. In Los Angeles, young chicanos (Mexican Americans) have been listening to straight up, electric guitar-driven rock and roll, either in English, Spanish, or Spanglish, for decades, and that city is now the main US locus of *rock en español*. Other young Chicanos prefer rap, which, like on the East Coast, includes rap made both by African Americans and Latinos. Recent Mexican immigrants to Los Angeles, on the other hand – of whom there are hundreds of thousands – prefer musics that originate in Mexico, such as *banda* and *corrido*.[2] In both the West and Southwest, salsa and merengue (and to a lesser extent, the newer bachata) are less prominent features of the Latino popular music landscape, although in that region, they are referred to collectively as *música tropical*, tropical music, to distinguish them from local Mexican-origin genres.

As for Miami, the city's soundscape is not dominated by the music of any one ethnic group. Once known as a bastion of (politically conservative) Cuban Americans, Miami's cultural demographics have been transformed by record numbers of immigrants from other Latin American countries, especially Colombia and Nicaragua. Moreover, because of its sizable Spanish-speaking population and its proximity to Latin America, the city has become the center of the Latin music and entertainment industries, which has had the effect of making Miami more diverse and musically cosmopolitan than other US cities where one ethnic/regional group predominates.

In short, the differences in musical preferences and practices among Latinos from the various regions of the US, between long-time residents and newer immigrants, as well as between young and old, are profound indeed, and express, in powerful ways unique to each community, how Latinos perceive themselves in relation to their sending societies, to other Latino communities, as well as to the larger US society of which they are now a constituent part. Clearly, referring to these diverse US musics, not to mention the numerous musics produced and consumed within Latin America, where the single term 'Latin music' is problematic, both because of its unmanageable reductionism, and because it perpetuates the exclusion of US Latinos from US cultural citizenship – i.e. as 'Americans.' I should note that the term *America* is even more problematic: it properly refers to the entire hemisphere, from Canada to Patagonia, but it has been coopted by the United States and reconstructed as a national, English-only category. The term has included blacks – a historically oppressed minority, to be sure – but far too often it has excluded those of Latin American ancestry, no matter how long they have resided in the US, and no matter how substantial their contributions to the cultural and economic fabric of the country has been. The operational assumption has been, if you are Latino, you are foreign, and therefore not 'American'.

The US music industry has balked at making any changes that would economically or even symbolically incorporate Latinos into what is considered 'American' music. This can be clearly observed in the attitudes of NARAS, the National Academy of Recording Arts and Sciences, the industry organization that awards the Grammies. In spite of the diverse regional Latino musics, each enjoying a vigorous regional market going back decades – salsa and Latin jazz in New York, conjunto and tejano in Texas, Chicano rock in California – the Grammy awards barely acknowledged the presence of Latino musics until 1975. For years, even as sales of musics made by and for Latinos were surpassing that of jazz and classical musics – both of which had Grammy awards – Latino musics were simply lumped into the 'ethnic and traditional' music category. It was not until public protests by New York Latinos that a Grammy for 'Latin music' was finally added in 1975.

NARAS rejected, however, the protesters' demands for multiple categories that would recognize and accommodate the diversity of Latin musics (Billboard 87: 8, May 3, 1975). It took another eight years – until 1983 – before NARAS was willing to increase the number of awards categories to three: one for Best Mexican American, one for Best Tropical, and another for Best Latin Pop. Another eight years later, in 1995 the Mexican-American Performance category was renamed as Best Mexican American/Tejano Performance, recognizing that tejano should not simply be subsumed under the Mexican American rubric. Finally, in 1998 this category was split again, into separate Tejano and Mexican American categories.

It took even longer for the Academy to recognize that the Tropical category was also an aesthetically and culturally untenable category: the category is scheduled to be split into two awards in 2000, one for salsa, another for merengue. As for rock, it was not until 1997 that NARAS added a Best Latin Rock/Alternative category – which can be considered progress in one regard, but it also raises the issue that rock identified as Latin is more likely to be considered a sub-set of Latin music than a sub-set of rock. In short, it has taken NARAS almost 25 years to recognize the cultural and regional specificities in 'Latin' music, all of which were there from the start. Moreover, I should note that until recently, the Latin music Grammies were (and mostly still are) awarded off-camera, guaranteeing that mainstream viewers will never be exposed to the musics in question.

In response to the steady growth of the Latin music industry as a whole, in September 2000 a new stand-alone Grammy committee – LARAS – hosted a gala award ceremony for Latin Grammies in Miami, with 39 categories, including four general awards such as record and artist of the year, and 12 other nomination fields, including pop, rock, tropical, regional, traditional, jazz, Brazilian, children's, classical, production and video. While again, in some respects this represents progress, it also runs the danger of perpetuating the segregation of Latin music from the industry mainstream. As journalist Fernando Gonzalez asks, '[W]ill Latin music in the US gain visibility in exchange for a separate-but-equal arrangement?' (1996). Or will separate turn out, as usual, to be unequal?

Aesthetic impacts of transnational migration on East Coast Latino music

Now I want to turn more attention to some of the aesthetic developments characterizing Latino musical production in the era of globalization. Globalization is usually thought of in terms of organized capital and telecommunications media that transcend national boundaries. Cultural products are recognized as important commodities in the globalization process, but much of what is happening in terms of the globalization of culture is the result of the flow of actual people moving and relocating – especially in cities – carrying with them an array of cultural baggage, from 'traditional' practices inherited from their ancestors, to whatever they may have picked up via the media in recent decades. Thus, the increased movement of people from multiple points of origin into cities is, as Sassen has pointed out, '. . . no less a part of globalization than is international finance' (1996: 186).

If considering the globalization of Latin/o popular music, one could legitimately focus on how the dissemination of Latin music has recently been expanded by the multinationals and telecommunications media. But an equally important aspect of the relationship between globalization and Latin music concerns the impact of new patterns of migration on the production and consumption of Latin/o popular music. Because of space limitations, I am going to restrict myself here specifically to the impact of immigration on US Latino popular music, rather than on Latin music in general.

Recent changes in the US Latino music landscape are without question the consequences of dramatically increased levels and new forms of immigration. In traditional patterns of migration, migrants' immediate links to the sending country are largely severed, and replaced with new connections to the receiving country; examples would be the early 20th century immigration to the US of Italians or Germans, who may have remained emotionally attached to the home country, but most – especially after the second generation – retained little direct contact with the sending region. A more recent example would be Cuban Americans, most of whom have been unable, for political reasons, to maintain meaningful contacts with Cuba and developments in Cuban culture.

Thanks to advances in telecommunications technology and transportation networks, more recent migrants are able to retain close and continuing contacts with their sending countries and its institutions, well into the second generation and perhaps further – it is too early to tell. Assimilation into the host society is no longer automatic nor is it even expected: if they so desire, immigrants can continue to participate actively in the economic, political and cultural life of the sending country, as well as in those of the receiving society. Puerto Ricans, who have been routinely traveling back and forth between the island and the US mainland since the 1940s, are the pioneers of these new patterns of circular migration (Flores 1996). More recently, other immigrant groups have been following suit, maintaining active links and participating directly with the specific villages and neighborhoods in Latin America from which they originated (e.g. Duany 1997, Levitt, in press). The cultural consequences of these new circumstances – on the Latin music industry as well as on the various Latino communities and their musical practices – are already proving themselves to be profound, as they are stimulating the reconfiguration of ethnic and racial identities, and redefining musical boundaries. Let me provide some examples:

In the 1980s, Dominicans began migrating to the US by the thousands (Pessar 1997). The majority have migrated to New York, although some also relocated in smaller northeastern seaboard cities such as Lawrence and Boston, Massachusetts and Providence, Rhode Island; many of them migrated to Puerto Rico as well, the latter a way station for Dominicans seeking eventual entrance to the US mainland (Duany 1997). Today, a full tenth of the Dominican Republic's population lives in the US – and this figure does not count the US-born children of Dominican parents. These growing diasporan communities have provided merengue, the Dominican Republic's most important genre of popular music, with important new markets outside the Dominican Republic itself (Austerlitz 1997). As merengue became more visible in the US, it began to supersede salsa in popularity, even among Puerto Ricans – salsa's primary practitioners – both in New York and on the island (Fernandez 1986). Nevertheless, throughout the 1980s most merengue was still being recorded and released in the Dominican Republic by Dominican labels, which were then exported to nostalgic Dominican expatriates in the US and in Puerto Rico.

Since the 1990s, however, the direction of flow has reversed, as the merengue industry's center of gravity has shifted from Santo Domingo to New York. According to a manager at J & N, currently the largest Dominican label, New York City now accounts for over three quarters of the company's merengue sales; the city also offers better-payng performance venues. The next largest market for merengue is Puerto Rico. The Dominican Republic itself, beset by extensive and chronic poverty, now accounts for a relatively small portion of the earnings derived from merengue sales and performance. As a result, many of the top merengue musicians have relocated to New York – although they continue to tour regularly in the Dominican Republic (Zuinda Lopez, personal communication). Interestingly, however, the most commercially successful merengue being produced today is being made by Puerto Rican musicians – a number of whom, it should be noted, are women (Duany 1998). This does not mean that the Dominican Republic is now irrelevant to merengue, but that the merengue business, like its performers and fans, has been dispersed to three distinct national and cultural settings – the Dominican Republic, Puerto Rico and the northeastern US. In short, the merengue, once the quintessential symbol of Dominican national identity, has been transformed into a transnational music no longer grounded in the Dominican Republic itself. Moreover, its most commercially successful musicians are no longer Dominican.

Perhaps more important than these structural changes are the aesthetic changes in the musics being made by and for Dominicans. Clearly, no matter how large and supportive an immigrant enclave can be, and how strong its connections to the homeland might be, its participants' location within the larger demographic realities of the US exerts a powerful counter force to immigrants' efforts to maintain the integrity of their cultural links to their homeland. In this regard, it important to note that when immigrants settle in the US, particularly in major receiving cities such as New York and Los Angeles, they do not encounter a monolithic 'American' culture, but rather a socio-cultural landscape that has always been diverse in terms of race, ethnicity and culture. Recent immigrants to cities such as New York and Los Angeles, for example, encounter not only the fictively-homogeneous white world represented in Hollywood films and television programming, but also large and well-established communities of African-Americans, Asians, and Central and South Americans, not to mention other Latinos who have lived in the US for generations, and who, in spite of their shared Latin American ancestry, are culturally quite distinct from the newcomers.

It is not surprising, then, that new styles have been emerging that reflect the experiences of a young generation of New York-born and/or -bred Dominicans who have grown up living and working next to African-Americans, Puerto Ricans, and other Latin American and Caribbean immigrants. US based groups such as Proyecto Uno, Los Ilegales, and Fulanito, composed of

Dominicans and Puerto Ricans, have been producing hybrids of merengue with salsa, rap, house and dancehall in English, Spanish and Spanglish, which have confounded the original boundaries of the various genres brought into the mix.

Purists have disdained this music as a commercial product lacking cultural authenticity. Clearly, such anxieties over musical borders reflect long-held and deeply-felt notions about the relationship between music and national identity: if merengue encapsulates *lo Dominicano*, who or what does *meren-rap* with Spanglish lyrics signify? In fact, these hybrids point directly to a generation of young Latino musicians and fans whose cultural roots are not located unambiguously in Latin America; instead, these young people have grown up living at the crossroads (to borrow Lipsitz' apt term [1994]) of the Latin American, Latino, black diasporan and anglo worlds, and their multiple (and often contradictory) identities are neatly and succinctly expressed by these musics' diverse cultural references.

Aesthetic impacts of transnational migration on West Coast Latino music

Examples from other parts of the US similarly reflect the same impact of transnational migration and transnational media on US Latino communities and their popular musics. Los Angeles, California, whose Latino population is primarily of Mexican rather than Spanish Caribbean descent, offers an especially useful comparison to New York. California has been home to people of Mexican descent since it was taken from Mexico in 1846; it has remained a favored destination for generations of immigrants from Mexico ever since. Mexican Americans born and raised in California have long participated in US popular musics of all sorts, but particularly rock and roll (cf. Lipsitz 1989, Guevara 1985, Loza 1993, Reyes and Waldbaum 1998). The list of Chicano rockers is long, from Ritchie Valens in the 1950s, Cannibal and the Headhunters in the 1960s, Carlos Santana in the 1970s, Los Lobos in the 1980s, to Rage Against the Machine's Zack de la Rocha in the 1990s. During the 1960s in particular, there was so much rock and roll being produced by Los Angeles Chicanos that it was recognized as a distinct style of rock and roll, the East Side Sound. Even with the rise of Chicano cultural nationalism during the 1970s, the rock and roll idiom was never rejected as something alien to Chicanos' cultural identity; instead, rock and roll was placed in the service of strengthening Chicano pride and self-empowerment via a variety of performance strategies, such as politicized lyrics (in both Spanish and English), and/or band names referring to Mexican culture (e.g. Azteca, El Chicano). As the 1970s proceeded, many Chicano musicians turned to punk (e.g. the Plugz), and later, in the 1980s, to rap (e.g. Kid Frost, Proper Dos,

Delinquent Habits). None of these musics, regardless of the ethnicity of the musicians or the language they used, were considered to be Latin music.

The arrival of massive numbers of immigrants from Mexico within the last two decades, however, has complicated the musical landscape of Latino Los Angeles. Some of the newcomers, those from northwestern Mexico, brought with them a style called banda, a music firmly rooted in the musical traditions of rural northwestern Mexico, with strong influences from German polka. As synthesizers, electric bass and trap drums were added to the traditional brass-based banda ensemble, along with performance styles borrowed from rock and roll, banda evolved into a new style that expressed the more cosmopolitan sensibilities of its now-urban musicians and fans. Nevertheless, young Mexican immigrants dancing to banda in Los Angeles clubs rejected the hip urban styles – baggy trousers, sneakers and baseball hats – preferred by their more acculturated native-born co-ethnics, insisting instead on wearing clothing that indexes their home culture – cowboy boots and hats, blue jeans, Western-style shirts, and large silver belt buckles bearing the emblem of their home state in Mexico. While the core of banda's fans are recent immigrants, some US-born Mexican Americans have also gravitated to banda, attracted by the strong sense of regional identity and cultural affirmation shared by its practitioners (Lipsitz 1999, Simonett 1996/97).

Like their Dominican counterparts, contemporary banda musicians work and live on both sides of the border – banda is still popular in rural northwestern Mexico – but the superior spending power of LA-based Mexicans has shifted banda's center of gravity to Los Angeles. As a result, while banda's aesthetics still symbolically invoke a rural Mexican homeland, it has been transformed into a fully modern, transnational music, whose financial center is urban Los Angeles.

Yet, even as banda was re-Mexicanizing the Latino popular music landscape of Los Angeles, US-born Chicanos, most of whom are bilingual, continued to prefer the music that had always been popular there – rock and roll. Interestingly, the increase of immigration from Mexico that stimulated the banda phenomenon also invigorated Los Angeles's traditional Chicano rock music scene. Many of the new immigrants relocating in Los Angeles hailed from urban, rather than rural, Mexico, and the musical preferences they brought from Mexico were for rock – both Mexican rock, in Spanish, which had been popular in Mexico for decades (see Zolov 1999), as well as the *rock en español* being produced in other Latin American countries, such as Argentina, Chile and Colombia. The sheer numbers of rock fans of Latin American origins residing in Los Angeles made it not only culturally acceptable but economically viable to make music in a language other than English. This encouraged young US-born bilingual Chicanos to begin producing rock in Spanish as well as English; the group Voodoo Glow Skulls, for example, released both English and Spanish versions of their CD *Firme* (Epitaph 86465-2).

Rock en español, I should note, is not identical to Chicano rock, which was primarily in English, and had always been an integral, if under-recognized, aspect of the larger US rock scene (cf. Garofalo 1997). *Rock en español*, in contrast, refers to the national rock traditions of Mexico, Argentina and other Latin American countries, and which as its name indicates, is always in Spanish. Early Latin American rock typically consisted of English-language covers of US hit parade material, but by the late 1970s and early 1980s, original rock with lyrics in Spanish about local concerns was being produced throughout Latin America and, as a group, being referred to as *rock nacional*. While the music of some *rock en español* musicians might be sonically indistinguishable from that of US and UK rockers, on the whole *rock en español* musicians tend to be more eclectic, drawing more freely from a variety of sources, from the national and folk music repertoires of their own country, to international styles such as reggae from the Caribbean, various sub-styles of rock and rap from the US, and soukous from Central/West Africa. Argentina's Fabulosos Cadillacs, Colombia's Bloque, Mexico's Cafe Tacuba, and Venezuela's Desorden Publico, for example, are producing unlikely combinations of rock, rap, reggae and ska with traditional national styles, as well as other Latin American and diasporan sources. Indeed, the recent success of *rock en español* among non-Latin/o Americans is being attributed to its fresh and innovative sounds.

Most Chicano rock musicians identify themselves as US rockers, preferring that their recordings be stocked in the 'rock' rather than the 'Latin' sections of music stores (where *rock en español* recordings are most likely to be found), but the eclecticism displayed by some of them place them aesthetically closer to their *rock en español* counterparts than to most contemporary US rockers, who on the whole are less experimental in their sound and sources.

In the late 1980s and early 1990s some young Chicanos began turning to rap as well. The first Chicano rapper to gain national visibility was Kid Frost, who had a hit single in 1990 called 'La Raza.' Kid Frosts' success was later surpassed by another LA-based rap group, Cypress Hill, which was multi-ethnic and multi-racial: a Mexican/Cuban American lead singer, an Afro-Cuban, and an Italian American. Behind these commercially-successful groups were and are dozens of others Chicano/Latino rap groups, such as Proper Dos, Delinquent Habits and Fifth Sun. Cypress Hill downplayed (but did not completely efface) its ethnicity and raps mostly in English, but other groups, such as Fifth Sun, whose name refers to an ancient Aztec prophecy, foreground their ethnic particularity in their choice of stage names (Cuatemóc, Makiuli and Chingon), rapping in Spanglish, and using samples from indigenous and traditional Latin musics.

A development related to these bi-lingual and bi-cultural musical styles is the increasing popularity of club DJs, who have been incorporating a range of styles from around the globe into an evening's performance – from salsa to reggae to house to Andean music to flamenco and beyond. The San Francisco-based Latino youth-oriented magazine *Frontera* calls this blending 'esoteric, post modern, or just straight up fresh,' but I have also heard the trend referred to as 'genre jumping' and as 'traveling music.' Popular as such sounds may be among the young, however, these developments are perceived by some to be threatening the integrity of formerly distinct categories of Latin music.

In short, increasing numbers of US Latino musicians have rendered national borders irrelevant by routinely marketing their recordings and live performance tours to their ethnic/national cohorts no matter where they live. More importantly, many of them are routinely crossing aesthetic borders as well, fusing their 'home' communities' traditional genres with others they have encountered in their host society, some of which are themselves transplants.

Conclusions

How do these eclectic new musics fit into the 'Latin music' category, and how do they challenge or confirm the cultural assumptions behind the music industry's marketing categories? So far, musics such as merengue and banda, whose roots if not its branches are clearly located in Latin America, are not immediately threatening the old order, since these musics, and most of those who make and consume them, can still be considered Latin American rather than native to the United States. This position, however, will not be tenable much longer: it is inevitable that the ever-widening cultural flows producing Latin/o musical hybrids, characterized by multiple sources and multiple performance locations, are going to destabilize the categories of 'Latin music' and 'American' music as they have been traditionally imagined.

Under these circumstances, one might reasonably argue that precisely because national borders *are* becoming increasingly irrelevant in the production and circulation of musics such as merengue and banda, the pan-national term 'Latin music' might be more appropriate than trying to impose artificial divisions between what is US-based and what is Latin American. Nevertheless, as long as the term Latin music continues to be used as it has historically been used – to separate out what is Latino from what is 'American,' it will continue to be problematic. Since it is not likely to disappear – and indeed, given the realities of globalization, since it might be useful to embrace the term – we should at least be aware of the noxious cultural assumptions that originally brought it into being, and avoid using it in an uncritical way.

Notes

1   On salsa, c. f. Aparicio 1998, Boggs 1992, Manuel 1994; on merengue, c. f. Austerlitz 1997; on bachata, c. f. Pacini Hernandez 1995; on Colombian cumbia and vallenato, c. f. Wade 2000; on Latino rap, c. f. Rivera 1996, Flores 1992-92; on Texas-Mexican music c. f. Peña 1999; on Chicano rock, c. f. Loza 1993, Lipsitz 1989; on Chicano rap, c. f. Kelley 1993, Corona 1997; on house music in Los Angeles, c. f. Karimi 1996; on banda, c. f. Lipsitz 1999, Simonnett, in press.

2   The distinctions between world music and world beat are not absolute, but in general, the world music category tends to privilege adherence to traditional musical practices and their concomitant auras of authenticity; world beat musics, in contrast, are rhythm-dominant (most are intended for dance floors), eclectic, fully modern, technologically-sophisticated musics that rely heavily on cross-fertilization of styles from multiple locations, but especially from throughout the African continent. The appeal of both world music and world beat musics to northern audiences has relied mainly on their perceived differences from Euro-American popular music – even though in the case of world beat, the aesthetic and technological distance from Western rock and pop is often relatively small. This may explain why Stapleton and May's 1990 book on contemporary Afropop styles (which clearly fall under the world beat umbrella) was entitled *African Rock: The Pop Music of a Continent.*

References

Aparicio, Frances (1998). *Listening to Salsa: Gender, Latin American Music and Puerto Rican Literature.* Hanover and London: Wesleyan University Press.

Austerlitz, Paul (1997). *Merengue: Dominican Music and Dominican Identity.* Philadelphia: Temple University Press.

Boggs, Vernon (1992). *Salsiology: Afro-Cuban Music and the Evolution of Salsa in New York City.* New York: Excelsior Publishing Co.

Burr, Ramiro (1999). 'Musicians Want Pact's Benefits.' *Express News*, May 11. (www.afm.org/depts/oe/star/starw3.htm)

Corona, Caprice (1997). *Representations of Ethnicity in the Chicano/Latino Rap Music and Hiphop Culture of Los Angeles,* California. Honors A. B. thesis, Harvard University.

Duany, Jorge (1984). 'Popular music in Puerto Rico: towards an anthropology of salsa.' *Latin American Music Review* 5 (2).

Duany, Jorge (1997). 'The creation of a transnational Caribbean identity: Dominican immigrants in San Juan and New York City.' In: Carrion, Manuel (ed.). *Ethnicity, Nationality and Race in the Caribbean.* Rio Piedras: Institute of Caribbean Studies, University of Puerto Rico.

Duany, Jorge (1998). 'Lo tengo dominao: el boom de las merengueras en Puerto Rico.' *Diálogo,* October.

Fernandez, Enrique (1986). 'Is salsa sinking?' *Village Voice,* September 2.

Flores, Juan (1992–3). 'Puerto Rican and Proud, Boyee.' *Journal of El Centro de Estudios Puertorriqueños,* Winter.

Flores, Juan (1996). 'Pan-Latino/Trans-Latino: Puerto Ricans in the "New Nueva York".' *Journal of El Centro de Estudios Puertorriqueños,* Spring.

Garcia, Jorge J. E. (2000). *Hispanic/Latino Identity: A Philosophical Perspective.* Malden, MA: Blackwell Publishers.

Garofalo, Reebee (1997). *Rockin' Out: Popular Music in the USA.* Boston: Allyn and Bacon.

Gonzalez, Fernando (1996). 'Latin Grammies: an idea whose time has come?' *Miami Herald* May 24.

Guevara, Ruben (1985). 'The view from the Sixth Street Bridge: The history of Chicano Rock.' In: Marsh, Dave (ed.). *Inside the Real World of Rock and Roll*. New York: Pantheon Books.

Karimi, Robert (1996). 'Wax alchemists.' *Frontera* 4.

Kelly, Raegan (1993). 'Hip hop Chicano: a separate but parallel story.' In: Cross, Brian (ed.) *It's Not About a Salary: Rap, Race and Resistance in Los Angeles*. New York: Verso.

Levitt, Peggy (in press). *The Transnational Villagers*. University of California Press.

Lipsitz, George (1989). 'Land of a thousand dances: youth, minorities, and the rise of rock and roll.' In: May, Larry (ed.) *Recasting America: Culture and Politics in the Age of Cold War*. Chicago: University of Chicago Press.

Lipsitz, George (1994). *Dangerous Crossroads: Popular Music, Postmodernism and the Poetics of Place*. New York: Verso.

Lipsitz, George (1999). 'Home is where the hatred is: work, music and the transnational economy.' In: Naficy, Hamid (ed.) *Home, Exile, Homeland: Film, Media and the Politics of Place*. New York and London: Routledge.

Loza, Steven (1993). *Barrio Rhythms: Mexican American Music in Los Angeles*. Urbana and Chicago: University of Illinois Press.

Manuel, Peter (1994). 'Puerto Rican music and cultural identity: creative appropriation of Cuban sources from danza to salsa.' *Ethnomusicology* 38 (2).

Negus, Keith (1999). *Music Genres and Corporate Cultures*. London and New York: Routledge.

Oboler, Suzanne (1995). *Ethnic Labels, Latino Lives*. Minneapolis: University of Minnesota Press.

Pacini Hernandez, Deborah (1995). *Bachata: A Social History of a Dominican Popular Music*. Philadelphia: Temple University Press.

Patterson, Rob (1999). 'Tejano blues and union dues support Tejano advancement in recording campaign.' *San Antonio Current*, May. (http://www.afm.org/depts/oe/star/star.htm)

Peña, Manuel (1999). *Música Tejana: The Cultural Economy of Artistic Transformation*. College Station: Texas A & M University Press.

Pessar, Patricia (1997). *Visa for a Dream*. Boston: Allyn and Bacon.

Reyes, David and Tom Waldbaum (1998). *Land of a Thousand Dances: Chicano Rock 'n' Roll from Southern California*. Albuquerque: University of New Mexico Press.

RIAA (Recording Industry Association of America) Online (1999). 'Hispanic Record Sales.' (http://www.riaa.com/stats/st_hrs.htm)

Rivera, Raquel (1996). 'Boricuas from the hip hop zone: notes on race and ethnic relations in New York City.' *Journal of El Centro de Estudios Puertorriqueños*, Spring.

Sassen, Saskia (1996). 'Rebuilding the Global City: Economy, Ethnicity and Space'. In: King, Anthony D. (ed.). *Re-Presenting the City: Ethnicity, Capital and Culture in the 21st-Century Metropolis*, New York: NYU Press, 1996.

Simonett, Helena (1996/97). 'Waving Hats and Stomping Boots.' *Pacific Review of Ethnomusicology* 8 (1): 41–49.

Simonett, Helena (in press). *Banda: Mexican Musical Life Across Borders*. Middletown, CT: Wesleyan University Press.

Stapleton, Chris and Chris May (1990). *African Rock: The Pop Music of a Continent*. New York: Dutton.

Taraska, Julie (1999). 'Latin music sales exploded in first half of '99.' *Billboard Daily Music Update*. (http://www.billboard.com/)

Wade, Peter (2000). *Music, Race and Nation: Musica Tropical in Colombia*. Chicago: University of Chicago Press.

Zolov, Eric (1999). *Refried Elvis: The Rise of the Mexican Counterculture*. University of California Press.

6 Popular music in ex-Yugoslavia between global participation and provincial seclusion

Alenka Barber-Kersovan

Though the music of ex-Yugoslavia[1] was always a subject of cultural exchange,[2] its reception by the international community on one hand and the dissemination of the global musical trends to this region on the other, were – and still are – inhibited by unfavourable framework conditions, under which at least the following four aspects have to be mentioned:

1. Socialistic production and distribution conditions between 1945 and 1989
2. The creation of nationalist barriers between different nations and nationalities after the mid eighties
3. The disintegration of the original state into the successor states Slovenia, Croatia, Bosnia and Herzegovina, Macedonia and Yugoslavia in 1991
4. Wars in Slovenia (1991), Croatia (1991/1992), Bosnia and Herzegovina (1992–1995) and Serbia (1999).

Rocking the socialistic state

The state known as the Socialist Federal Republic of Yugoslavia was founded in 1943. In spite of chronic economic problems, in comparison with other socialistic countries the living standard was high. There was a relatively high degree of freedom of expression, a well-developed media-scape, a lively flow of information across the open borders as well as a political climate which fostered the cultural sphere with generous subsidies, qualified artist education and high appreciation of cultural work. There was also a number of well-established international cultural events such as the Graphic Biannual in Ljubljana, the Bitef film festival in Belgrade and the Summer Festival in Dubrovnik, which were attended by artists from the East and the West.

Popular music did not belong to the cultural sphere. It operated outside the system of cultural subsidies and thus also outside the immediate grip of state control, obeying the laws of a chaotic music market. Thus, for instance, contrary to the German Democratic Republic (cf. Rauhut 1993), there were no bureaucratic restrictions on who could perform publicly, who could travel abroad, who could import instruments, which foreign group could be invited and which not, and also repression of the Western style of 'fanism' was rather moderate. But there were also no fixed wages, no appropriate social or medical security for the musicians and no appropriate educational possibilities (cf. Barber-Kersovan 1998a).

Also the Yugoslav music industry was never centralized as in other socialistic countries. Instead, there was a number of bigger and smaller record companies, whereby the majors were either independent 'working organizations' (Jugoton, Diskoton) or they were attached to the republican radio and television stations. Furthermore, there was a lot of musical import and licensed editions. Vice versa however, in spite of its overt commercial orientation, the Yugoslav music industry did very little to promote its artists abroad: Musicians and groups who made an international career were coached by Western agents and firms. The Folk-like Ensemble Slavko Avsenik, for instance, was marketed by the German media and the German record industry, and the group Laibach has a contract with Mute Records.

Unlike in other socialistic countries, independent labels also existed in Yugoslavia, promoting bands from the musical underground. Yet contrary to the West, where independents were small commercial enterprises, these labels were parts of existing social structures, mostly student cultural organizations, institutions or alternative media, such as Radio Student or the Student Cultural Centre in Ljubljana. In this segment of the musical life, especially during the eighties, there was a lot of international co-operation, so that, for instance, the Hard Core community in Ljubljana operated predominantly in the framework of the 'Hard Core International' and the 'Maximum Rock'n'-Roll'.

Yugo-Rock

As all communist regimes, also Yugoslav self-government defined itself in opposition to the capitalist West and was at the ideological level rather suspicious about what was labelled 'Americanization', 'cultural imperialism' and the 'import of Western decadence'. Nevertheless, under the economic conditions described, the recontextualization of Anglo-American pop music in ex-Yugoslavia was not dissimilar to other moderately developed industrial countries and thus by the mid seventies, there was already an 'authentic rock and pop climate', encompassing aspects such as the mass production and mass consumption of popular music and related goods, the development of genuine rock rituals, the coming-up of the pop music press and criticism as well as the creation of typical songs based on the fusion of Rock 'n' Roll and the local musical traditions (cf. Tuksar 1978: 10 ff).

Most of the well-known acts came from the republican capitals, Ljubljana, Zagreb, Belgrade and Sarajevo, which – due to different historical, political, religious and cultural backgrounds – had rather different musical scenes (cf. Janjatovic 1998). But – contrary to the Folk-like music, which was bound to certain cultural environments – there was a country-wide market for domestic Rock 'n' Roll. 'Big groups' had their fans in different settings, irrespective of their 'national' or 'ethnic' origin, so that in 1978 the group Bijelo dugme from the Bosnian capital Sarajevo was still cheered in the Serbian capital Belgrade by some 100,000 fans.

Bijelo dugme, one of the most commercially successful as well as artistically refined groups of the late seventies, was known as the founder of a musical style called 'Yugo-Rock' with numerous references to Balkan 'melos' (i. e. characteristic scales, instruments, guttural singing style, rhythmic structures, etc.; cf. Tomc 1998: 41). Furthermore, Bijelo dugme was also known as a pro-Yugoslav group which correctly diagnosed the political situation during the mid eighties and put their opinions into numerous songs. An example is the title 'Spit and Sing My Yugoslavia' from the year 1986, in which with the lines 'Get up and sing, my Yugoslavia! Who is not listening to the song will hear the thunder', the group pleaded for a peaceful resolution of the situation.

Similar to Bijelo dugme, Plavi orkestar also came from Sarajevo. Becoming popular under the name The Balkan Beatles,[3] Plavi orkestar played a revival style of Yugo-Rock, called 'New Primitivism' or 'Balkan Folklorism'. 'We are Folk-like musicians', the group claimed. 'We are glorifying the Folk and the Folk culture' (Gracanin 1985: 47). Also this group expressed their worries about the political developments. One of the most outstanding and significant numbers is 'You Are Not Supposed to Be a Fascist', about the Second World War, as parts of the Muslim community were collaborating with the German occupiers. The message of this gloomy love song, in which a Muslim girl is accused of dating 'a blond Hitler's son', was 'You are not supposed to be a fascist dear, because otherwise I am going to kill you'.

The disintegration of the communal music market

Both songs and especially the militant iconography of the record covers gave a foretaste of the events to come. Since the Yugoslav state was predominantly an administrative unit, controlling economy, finances, defence and external politics, culture and education were republican domains. But there were also strong efforts to create a 'Yugoslav nation' on the basis of the 'brotherhood and unity of the Yugoslav nations and nationalities' (cf. Wachtel 1998). Musically, this political goal was put into practice in manifestations such as the meetings of the jazz orchestras of the republican radio and television stations, rock competitions such as YURM (*Jugoslovanski rock momenat*; Yugoslav Rock Moment) and pop song contests like The Festival of Opatija or The Split Summer, at which the juries made sure that the prices were equally distributed among the republics. Folklore festivals were also very popular during the mid eighties, and traditional music and dances from all parts of the country were presented.

With the growing national tensions from the mid eighties onwards, similarly to all other parts of the public life, the music began to shut itself off behind republican and ethnical boundaries (cf. Dragicevic-Sesic, in: Slosar 1997: 130). Multinational groups fell apart and the federal music events mentioned above lost their importance (cf. Janjatovic 1998). Also the musical repertoire changed significantly. Partisan songs were swept under the carpet along with other musical pieces which did not conform to the new spirit of nationalism. The media broadcast predominantly Anglo-American pop music or songs by regional or local bands; groups once celebrated as Yugoslav stars were confined to playing in their own environments and they seldom got a deal with a record company in another republic: The multicultural soundscape broke down into a number of monocultural soundscapes with stronger or weaker references to the global musical trends.

Creating psychological barriers

The answer to the question of whether the disintegration of ex-Yugoslavia was due to the historical animosities between different nations and nationalities, the collapse of socialism, the struggle for power between the nationalistic elites or the Serbian expansionist politics should be left to the historians (cf. Furkes & Schlarp 1991; Fritzler 1993; Glenny 1993; Jez 1995; Heuberger & Riegler & Vidovic 1999). The fact however is that – following the 'implosion of socialism' (Altermatt 1996: 239) in 1989 – a political, territorial, religious and cultural fragmentation began, breaking the federation into a number of small, self-centred units. History was rewritten along nationalistic lines, memories of the socialistic past were extinguished and the ideology of the 'brotherhood and unity of the Yugoslav nations and nationalities' was replaced by the paradigm that different ethnic groups cannot live in a communal state (cf. Stojanovic, in Slosar 1997: 225).

Musicians had to adjust to the new situation (cf. Buric, in: Pieper 1999: 104). Some of them changed their profession, some chose exile,[4] so that especially in London there is a strong community of recent musical emigrants from all parts of ex-Yugoslavia. Some musicians however, predominantly in Croatia and Serbia, let themselves be instrumentalized by the new political power holders and were actively involved in creating psychological barriers between an imaginary 'Us' and 'Them'. Characteristic of their massive song production was the archetypal enlarging of the differences between the individual national groups by picturing the positive image of self as being 'good', 'always right' and 'a tragic victim of the circumstances', and 'the others' as being 'bad', 'wrong' and 'aggressors' (cf. Pesic & Rosandic, in: Slosar 1997: 220).

The musical construction of nationalistic ideology in Serbia

The most bizarre production of this kind came from Serbia. Here in an atmosphere which was – and still is – extremely hostile to everything coming from the West,[5] international rock and pop music has been pushed to the margins. There is still a kind of a rock scene and there are also some examples of deployment of this musical genre for political propaganda.[6] But in general, especially during the early nineties, the collectivist ideology of nationalism - was forged along the lines of myths, symbols and rituals on the basis of the local cultural traditions.

The Serbian regime presented itself as populist, a rurally oriented nationalistic elite replacing the urban-oriented Communist elite. The key word of this retrograde orientation was 'newly composed' which applied to all and everything, including the 'Newly Composed Folk Song'.[7] Under almost pathologically ethnocentric conditions, this musical genre, which already transported a rather conservative message, adopted a previously unknown fusion of myths and politics or a musical presentation of politics as folklore (cf. Burkhart, in: Colovic 1993: 8). In this connection the radio station Ponos radio (Radio Pride), established in 1992, has to be mentioned. It broadcast Folk and Newly Composed Folk Music 24 hours a day, mostly songs with political, patriotic or militaristic texts (cf. Colovic 1993: 87 ff). A fancier variant of this genre is an eclectic Dance/Folk melange, known as 'Turbo Folk', aiming at the populist urban population.

The most important topos of these songs is the glorification of the *ideologem* of Serbian nationalism (cf. Burkhart, in: Colovic 1993: 8), the myth of Kosovo. This myth is about the battle of Kosovo in 1389, when the Serbs lost the fight with the Turks and came under Ottoman rule, under which they stayed until 1877, when Serbia became an independent kingdom (cf. Fritzler 1993: 13 ff). In the 'patriotic' songs described, these historical events were recycled as if they were a part of the existing conditions, lacking any critical distance or historical perspective. The current political situation was pictured as fate and the politicians in power as fictional figures, descending from what was considered to be the 'heroic past', so that legend, imagination and reality fused into a timeless ritual, disconnected from the actual events.

The strength of the ties between this neo-folkloristic fundamentalism and actual politics was shown by the marriage of the commander of the paramilitaries Zeljko Raznatovic, known as Arkan,[8] to the star of the Neo-Folk scene Svetlana Celickovic-Ceca. The video of their wedding, which was staged as a mega-concert with the local celebrities of this genre, became a best-seller. Just as a footnote it must be mentioned that in the divided Bosnian town of Mostar this video was played outdoors for days at maximum volume in order to upset the Croatians living on the other side of the river (cf. Buric, in: Pieper 1999: 102).

'Music went to war' in Croatia

Between 1991 and 1999, four wars were fought on the territory of ex-Yugoslavia. As different as their political reasons, historical backgrounds and military outcomes might have been, except for the ten-days war between the Yugoslav Army and the Slovenian territorial defence, all conflicting parties were engaged in military music production. The first example concerns the Croatian war (1991/1992) following the declaration of Croatia as an independent state. The armed conflict broke out in the Croatian region of Krajina, where the majority of the population was Serb. Once treated as equal citizens of the Yugoslav state, at the Croatian declaration of independence, the 600,000 Serbs of this region became an ethnic minority which was denied its basic human rights (cf. Glenny 1993: 33 ff).

In comparison to Serbian political propaganda, in Croatia the aesthetic representation of the state power was to a lesser extent based on folkloristic populism: The main influence was Western popular culture. The marketing of ideology followed the mechanisms of a modern media society; political rituals were staged as media shows; and the task of transporting political messages through music was frequently taken over by Rock and Pop bands (cf. Cale-Feldman, in: Cale-Feldman et al. 1993: 5 ff) who played the Croatian version of 'Global Beat' which had been promoted by the highly developed Croatian music industry during the socialistic era.

These mechanisms became particularly evident during the war, when a special kind of War Art (cf. Senjkovic, in: Cale-Feldman et al. 1993) appeared, encompassing forms of visual expression such as stickers, badges and poster design. The War Art iconography was based on the symbolism of the national identity, and the messages included slogans like 'Help Croatia', 'We want to be free' and 'Stop the war in Croatia', very often in English. Produced in innumerable copies, these War Art items blurred the demarcation line between political propaganda and commercial war kitsch, turning the bloody front events[9] into television entertainment.

In a similar way, the semantics of war was also propagated through music. The most significant songs of this type have been documented by Croatian television in a video with the title 'For the Freedom' featuring prominent musicians. In order to strengthen the effects of the music, the same political slogans hammered into the consciousness of the public by the War Art were inserted between the clips.

In this post-modern mix of different musical styles three topoi were dominant. The first depicts the Croatians in the role of the victims. Visually, the emotional foil of this topos is based on the aesthetics of destruction, mingling stage scenery with snapshots of war destruction. Further ingredients are scenes of suffering and anguish resembling reality TV, portraying the old and the weak, crying children and newly born babies which need to be protected.

The second topos concerns the religious connotation of this war. Since religion and ethnos seem to be inseparable items in the Balkans, in the events discussed all conflicting groups based their cultural identity on myths and symbols that were derived from a Catholic, Orthodox or Muslim spiritual background (cf. Altermatt 1996: 121). In the video discussed, this issue, the Catholic roots of the Croatian identity, was expressed musically in an expressive Blues with the title 'Santa Maria'. Destroyed churches and graveyards were chosen as the setting, and such scenes provided the sole visual background of the video for the song 'For Whom the Bell Tolls'.

The third topos deals with the romanticization and glorification of the war. 'Our horizon is the front' and 'Also the Punx are defending Croatia', screamed the Punk group Psihomodo pop in order to make the official slogan 'Croatia has to win' palatable to the youngsters.[10] The alternative intelligentsia, on the other hand, was addressed by the title 'Say Yo for Croatia' by the dance-theatre group Montazstroj and the frontman HC Boxer. The hard electro-industrial sound of this number was underlined with the following text:

> *Montazstroj & HC Boxer:*
> *'Croatia in Flames'*
>
> Say Yo for Croatia.
> Say No for the war.
>
> Croatia is in flame,
> Our holy motherland.
> Suffering, bleeding, humiliated.
> Desperate, in pain.
> There is no time to hesitate,
> No time to waste.
>
> Take your arms, join your hands,
> Defeat the enemy.

> This is the time of glory,
> The time of final victory.
>
> Fight, fight, fight!
> Fight now!
>
> *(Transcribed from the video)*[11]

The fact that – as in the example above – almost half of the songs in the video 'For the Freedom' were written in English had a number of different reasons. Since the Band Aid project was realized at the same time Croatia was making desperate efforts to become acknowledged as a sovereign state, the message of these songs was not addressed to the Croatians only, but also to the international community. Another aspect considers the self-image of Croatia in terms of a Westernized, modern European country. Thus in an atmosphere in which everything that had the slightest hint of being 'Balkanesque' was forcefully suppressed (cf. Pettan 1996), the use of English signalled on the linguistic level that the country was trying to blow all bridges to the nations which were treated as 'brothers' before.

The extent to which the country at war dreamt a 'European dream' is made evident by a song in which the souls of the dead soldiers were compared with the 'golden stars' that were supposed to 'reappear on the blue sky of the European flag'. The song 'Stop the War in Croatia' (cf. Pettan, in Pettan 1998: 24) also belongs in the same context. In this sentimental video scenes from different Croatian regions were combined with spots from television news, featuring political events like President Tudjman's visits with the Pope and the German Chancellor Kohl. This song became an unofficial hymn of gatherings and demonstrations at which Croatian citizens appealed to 'Europe' to end the conflict, if necessary, with force:

Tomislav Ivcic: 'Stop the War in Croatia'

> Stop the war in the name of love,
> Stop the war in the name of God,
> Stop the war in the name of children,
> Stop the war in Croatia.
>
> We want to share the European dream,
> We want to share democracy and peace.
> Let Croatia be one of Europe's stars.
> Europe, you can stop the war.

(Transcribed from the video)

'Rock under Siege'

In 1992 the Bosnian war started. The political problem behind the military encounter was due to the fact that three nationalistic parties, the Serbian, the Croatian and the Muslim, won the first democratic elections by fuelling the tensions between the ethnical groups. With the recognition of Bosnia and Herzegovina as an independent state, these tensions turned into fierce fighting (cf. Achenbach 1994: 155), whereby next to the catchwords like 'Gorazde' and 'Srebrenica', our television memories embrace the dramatic siege of the Bosnian capital Sarajevo by the Serbian paramilitaries.

In the past, due to its multicultural social structure, Sarajevo had the image of a 'small Yugoslavia'. It was a lively, tolerant and inspiring urban center, hosting some of the best Yugo-Rock bands. During the two years lasting siege, urban life, including culture, came to an almost complete standstill.[12] And yet, paradoxical as it might seem, some 30 new rock groups were formed (cf. Basin 1997: 21) under impossible living conditions (cf. Dizdarevic 1995) and in spite of the constant shelling of the city. 'At the time of the siege you had the choice: Either you burn your furniture or you make out of it drumsticks', explained a musician. 'We made drumsticks. Rock music was the only chance to live out our energies' (quoted after Seidel-Pielen 1996). So youngsters risked their lives to come to the clubs in order to listen to the bands playing contemporary musical genres with no 'Balkan inspirations'. For them, 'Global Beat' had a vital function of a counterbalance to cold, hunger, national hatred and war primitivism.

This scene gathered around the radio station Radio zid, meaning Radio Wall, which was founded in 1992 in order to break down the invisible, but nevertheless firmly established, barriers between individuals of different cultural and religious convictions (cf. http://www.cyvezid.com). This independent radio station featured news and information, social affairs, culture and music, whereby especially the show Ex-Yu Pop Rock Links with its memories of the golden times of Yugo-Rock was extremely popular. Furthermore, Radio zid's productions encompassed sound and video recordings as well as the organization of concerts called 'Rock under Siege' (cf. Basin 1997: 20).

Due to the political involvement of the international community, the - Bosnian war received much broader international media coverage than those in Slovenia and Croatia.[13] Also the musical scene around Radio zid was paid a lot of attention, especially by MTV, which even took up the role of a musical war reporter. Characteristic of these rockumentaries called Sarajevo Special was that they did not focus their attention on suffering, death and destruction, but on the signs of life in a dead city. For young Bosnians, the fact that MTV portrayed music-loving youngsters rather than anonymous masses of war victims and refugees was understood as a sign of recognition.

They could not physically leave the city, but they had the feeling that regardless of the circumstances they remained members of the world-wide MTV nation (cf. Hujic 1996).

The bombing campaign

Between March and June 1999, NATO launched a bombing campaign over - Serbia, Kosovo and Montenegro. Since the media played a crucial role (cf. Jez 1995: 48; Baringhorst et al. 1995; Bugarski, in: Slosar 1997: 107 ff) in all conflicts discussed, the bombing campaign too was accompanied by a fierce media fight between NATO, which destroyed infrastructures, jammed frequencies, broadcast its version of the truth and pressed Eutel to remove Serbian television from the satellite on one side, and the Serbian propaganda machine on the other. Thus, for instance, Serbian television broadcast defamatory video spots with messages such as 'Albanians are drug dealers' and 'Clinton is a fascist', shows praising the heroism of the Yugoslav army underlined by 'patriotic songs', historical films about the partisans fighting against the Germans in the Second World War, and the film *Wag the Dog*, a parody of a fictional American president leading a nonsensical war with Albania.

Though in Serbia everything 'American', 'Western' or 'international' had to be ridiculed or condemned,[14] it is a paradox that – in musical terms – this war will not be remembered by the neo-traditionalism of the Newly Composed Folk songs, but by the Rock concerts which were performed on Belgrade's main square under the motto 'The song kept us going'.[15] Also in other countries, initiatives disapproving of the bombing campaign deployed Rock music as a means of symbolic resistance, so that for a short time Serbian Rock and Pop music experienced not only an enormous popularization, but also an international exchange unknown beforehand. Foreign bands were playing in Belgrade, and Serbian bands were touring abroad, such as Bajaga i instruktori, which performed with Russian stars in Moscow, or one of the veterans of Yugo-Rock, Goran Bregovic, who was the hype of the May Day celebrations in Rome (cf. Borba, May 1, 1999). Feedback even came from countries as far away as China. 'Now you see, Rock'n'Roll is not only amusement, but also a kind of power', announced the Rock China Forum on its home page. 'Let's go hand in hand to support the justice and denounce the evil'.

'Keep on Rockin' in the Free World' with 'Free B92'

Due to martial law and the political censorship, all Serbian opposition media were silenced during the bombing campaign. Among them was also the Belgrade student radio station B92. Launched in 1989 as a politically independent alternative to the government-run radio and TV stations, B92 was founded on the principles of the Declaration of Human Rights. Next to broadcasting devoted to rock music and politics, the activities of this 'young' radio station included publishing of printed matter; music, video and television production; and operation of a cultural center. Further, B92 is the core of ANEM, the Association of Independent Electronic Media in Yugoslavia. For its commitment to human rights, tolerance and respect for (ethnic) minorities, B92 was honoured with a number of prestigious international awards, including the Olof Palme Memorial Fund Award and the MTV Free Your Mind Award.

During the first days of the war, B92 was sealed off, the staff was sent home and the chief producer was arrested. The radio station was then taken over by a youth organization loyal to the regime which started to broadcast news from the state news agency. 'Global Beat', predominantly jazz, alternative rock, HipHop, Drum&Bass, House and Techno, was replaced by Serbian, Russian and Greek folklore.

The original collaborators, however, went underground. 'When reality fails us, we move to the virtual world' was the motto of the 'New B92' which started to broadcast via the Internet: The tiny radio station, which a couple of years ago could be heard in Belgrade only, became a global player with mirror sites in Europe, USA and Australia. Furthermore, radio majors such as BBC and ORF gave it a hand by transforming Real Audio files into radio signals and broadcasting them back to Serbia via satellite. In a protest against the war, B92 also initiated a number of musical events, such as a 24-hour Global Music Peace Netcast, in which prominent DJs, musicians and groups from all over the world were participating. This event was co-ordinated from Vienna by ORF Kunstradio.

Conclusions

Considering the issue of globalization, from the examples sketched, the following conclusions can be drawn:

1. After the Second World War, the complexity of social interactions in ex-Yugoslavia, including music, has been constructed along the division lines between 'Us' and 'Them'. Who or what has been included in or who or what has been excluded from a certain cultural in-group, however, varied over ti ne according to the prevailing economic, social and political conditions.

2. In different settings and at different times different social groups participated in the international exchange of cultural goods under different conditions and in a number of different ways. This exchange affected
   - macro systems (national states versus the global/international community)
   - meso systems (relationships between the individual states on the territory of ex-Yugoslavia)

- micro systems (subcultural circles, independent media networks, Internet groups).

3. The international exchange of cultural goods in ex-Yugoslavia and its successor states is asymmetric: Although 'Global Beat' has been recontextualized to a degree that it can serve also as a construction means for the national or even nationalistic identity (Croatia), the music from this part of the world is hardly known to the international community.

4. The orientation towards the local or the global musical experience varies from claustrophobic self-centeredness to cosmopolitanism or from retrograde traditionalism to high-tech modernity such as in the case of the Cyber Media Lab in Novi Sad.

5. Populist (musical) trends are paradoxical phenomena, because even in cases where the 'sounds' are neo-traditional, the forms of musical presentation (video clips, media distribution, record production, Internet presentation) are based on the international technological standards.

6. In the events discussed, commercial aspects seemed to play a secondary role. The level of global participation or provincial seclusion was rather determined by political, cultural and psychological variables.

7. It is highly regrettable that music from this region gained moderate resonance in the global community less for its musical characteristics ('Balkan melos') or musical quality (Yugo-Rock) than for the sensational setting (war, ethnic cleansing) it was imbedded into.

Notes

1   The territory of ex-Yugoslavia encompassed the republics Slovenia, Croatia, Bosnia and Herzegovina, Serbia with its until 1989 autonomous provinces Vojvodina and Kosovo, Montenegro and Macedonia. In 1991 the population numbered approximately 22,000,000.

2   In this connection at least the numerous musicians which are a part of the international art scene (Marjana Lipovsek, Vinko Globokar, Ivo Pogorelic), the participation at international festivals and competitions (Eurovision Song Contest), the music of the guest workers and immigrants as well as the role of the music in the once flourishing Adria tourism have to be mentioned.

3   At its best times, Plavi orkestar was selling millions of records, and the group also had some success abroad, especially in Russia and Algeria. Now the band's leader, Sasa Losic-Loso, is living in Slovenia, and in 1997 he even represented this country in the Eurovision Song Contest (cf. Virant 1998: 25 ff).

4   The once spoiled and also financially well-off Yugoslav pop stars rarely achieve real success in the West. A rare exception is Kolja, the leader of the Serbian group Disciplina kicme, whose new Disciplin-A-Kitschme is the shooting star of the London underground. Kolja, known as the 'Jimmy Hendrix of the bass guitar', changed his style from Yugo-Rock to minimalist Drum&Bass, but did not deny his musical roots (cf. http://www.demon.co.uk/disciplin/them.html; cf. also Janjatovic 1998).

5   The rejection of 'American' or 'Eurocentric' attitudes is the dominant trait of the Serbian New Right cultural politics. The UN embargo, including the exchange of cultural goods, reinforced this trend (cf. Dragicevic-Sesic, in: Slosar 1997: 137–138).

6   In this connection it should be mentioned that the daughter of President Milosevic owns a
     radio and television station (Kosava) which has the pretension of becoming the 'Serbian
     MTV' and that his son is running a chain of discotheques as well as the radio station Ma-
     dona.

7   Accompanying the extensive industrialization and the mass migration from the country
     into the towns, this musical genre appeared during the fifties in a number of different, re-
     gionally coloured variants (cf. Doliner 1978; Povrazanovic 1983: 776). Featuring pre-
     dominantly local artists, the Newly Composed Folk Song always had as many or even
     more fans than Anglo-American pop music.

8   Arkan, who was wanted by Interpol for his supposed involvement in a number of rob-
     beries as well as by the War Tribunal in Den Haag as a war criminal, was shot dead in
     January, 2000 by unknown killers (cf. Walker, 2000).

9   The strength of Western popular culture's influence on the war is showed by the follow-
     ing examples: 1) The image of the first 'defenders of Croatia' resembled the image of
     rock fans. They wore earrings, Ray Ban glasses, jeans, tennis shoes, T-shirts with differ-
     ent messages (in English) and very often a Punk hair cut. 2) The combat formations fre-
     quently had (English) names like The Tigers, The Yellow Ants, The Storms, Cheerful
     Cupboards, The Killing Medical Corps, Scorpions or The Garfields that resembled the
     names of the rock bands. 3) An alternative radio station from Osijek was called Yellow
     Submarine and also its jingle was adopted from the well-known song by the Beatles (cf.
     Hadzihusejnovic-Valasek, in: Pettan 1998: 170).

10   This title was also intended to fuel the spirit of the soldiers. Davor Gobac, the frontman
     of the group, explained: 'We recorded a true Punk piece with which I hope to stimulate
     the blood of the guardsmen on the front lines to circulate faster, to upgrade their morale.
     . . . The video clip was made for those who fight rather than for those who sit at home and
     watch TV. I just hope that they have the opportunity to see it in the intervals between bat-
     tles' (quoted after Pettan, in: Pettan 1998: 14).

11   In spite of its militant message, this video was shown also on MTV (cf. Prica, in: Cale-
     Feldman et al. 1993: 48–49).

12   Similar to the situation in Croatia, where everything that sounded 'Serbian' was banned
     during the early nineties (cf. Buric, in: Pieper 1999: 101), music in Bosnia was 'ethnical-
     ly cleansed'. Thus, for instance, before the national tensions exaggerated, all three ethnic
     groups, the Serbs, the Croats and the Muslims, appreciated, performed and consumed the
     urban love song 'Sevdalinka'. Under the tense political conditions, however, 'Sevdalin-
     ka' was appropriated by the Muslims as the musical symbol of their cultural identity and
     was consequently banned from the music repertoire of other ethnic groups (cf. Bajrekta-
     revic, in: Reuer 1999: 155 ff).

13   The Bosnian war also found numerous aesthetic reinterpretations in other countries. In
     this connection next to the Benetton shock-advertising campaign, showing a blood
     soaked uniform of a killed Bosnian soldier (cf. Baringhorst et. al., 1995: 98 ff), at least
     the LP *NATO* by the Slovenian group Laibach or the song 'The Train from Dachau to Sa-
     rajevo' by Mental Obsessions of Stuttgart, who visualized their electronic neo-industrial
     tortures with offensive pictures, superimposing scenes from German concentration
     camps and 'ethnically cleansed' Bosnian villages, have to be mentioned.

14   In this connection especially television spots have to be mentioned, expressing anti-
     American or anti-European feelings by turning the NATO logo into a swastika.

15   As Rock music is a 'symbol of modernism' or 'one of the pillars of cultural globalization
     and homogenization' (Mursic, in: Mursic & Brumen 1999: 139), it is another paradox of
     this war that – after this symbolic kind of resistance received broad coverage in the West-
     ern media – the organization of these concerts has been taken over by the Serbian author-
     ities as a part of their propaganda strategy.

References

Achenbach, Marina (1994). *Auf dem Weg nach Sarajevo*. Berlin: Elefanten Press.

Altermatt, Urs (1996). *Das Fanal von Sarajevo. Ethnonationalismus in Europa*. Zurich: Verlag Neue Zürcher Zeitung.

Barber-Kersovan, Alenka (1998a). 'The Issue of Performance in a System of the Socialistic Selfgovernment.' In: Hautamaki, Tarja & Jarvilouma, Helmi (eds.). *Music on Show. Issues of Performance*. Dept. of Folk Tradition Publ. Nr. 25. Tampere: University of Tampere Printing Service, 18–22.

Barber-Kersovan, Alenka (1998b). 'Wie das Fremde eigen wurde und das Eigene fremd. (Pop)Musikalische Streifzüge durch einige Republiken des ehemaligen Jugoslawiens.' In: Gruhn, Wilfried (ed.). *Musik anderer Kulturen. 10 Vorträge und ein Resümee zu interkulturellen Ansätzen in Musikwissenschaft und Musikpädagogik*. Kassel: Gustav Bosse Verlag.

Baringhorst, Siegrid & Müller, Bianca & Schmied, Holger (eds.) (1995). *Macht der Zeichen – Zeichen der Macht. Neue Strategien politischer Kommunikation*. Frankfurt etc.: Lang.

Basin, Igor (1997). 'Sarajevo ima kulturo.' *Muska*. Nr. 8, 20–25.

Bielefeld, Uli (ed.) (1991). *Das Eigene und das Fremde. Neuer Rassismus in der Alten Welt*. Hamburg: Jubius.

Borba: http://www.borba.co.yu/daily.html

Bornewasser, Manfred & Wakenhut, Roland (eds.) (1999). *Ethnisches und nationales Bewußtsein. Zwischen Globalisierung und Regionalisierung*. Frankfurt etc.: Lang.

Brey, Thomas (1993). *Die Logik des Wahnsinns. Jugoslawien – von Tätern und Opfern*. Freiburg, Basel, Vienna: Herder Spektrum.

Cale-Feldman, Liana & Prica, Ines & Senjkovic, Reana (eds.) (1993). *Fear, Death and Resistance. An Ethnography of War. Croatia 1991–92*. Zagreb: Institute of Ethnology and Folklore Research.

Colovic, Ivan (1993). *Bordell der Krieger. Folklore, Politik und Krieg*. Osnabrück: Fibre.

Disciplin-A-Kitschme: http://www.demon.co.uk/disciplin/them.html

Dizdarevic, Zlatko (1995). *Der Alltag des Krieges. Ein Tagebuch aus Sarajevo*. Frankfurt/New York: Campus Verlag.

Doliner, Gorana (1978). 'Folklor i novokomponirana narodna muzika.' *Zvuk* Nr. 1. 20–24.

Fritzler, Marc (1993). *Das ehemalige Jugoslawien*. Munich: Wilhelm Heyne Verlag.

Furkes, Josip & Schlarp, Karl-Heinz (1991). *Jugoslawien. Ein Staat zerfällt*. Reinbek bei Hamburg: Rowohlt.

Giesen, Bernd (1991). *Nationale und kulturelle Identität. Studien zur Entwicklung des kollektiven Bewußtseins in der Neuzeit*. Frankfurt: Suhrkamp Taschenbuch Wissenschaft.

Glenny, Misha (1993). *Jugoslawien. Der Krieg, der nach Europa kam*. München: Knaur.

Gracanin, Tomi (1985). 'Plavi orkestar.' *Mladina* 25.IV, 47.

Gracanin, Tomi (1987). 'Plavi orkestar: Smrt fasizmu.' *Mladina* 13.II, 44.

Greverus, Ina-Maria (1995). 'Reden oder Schweigen? Über einen ethno-anthropologischen Umgang mit dem Krieg.' *Zeitschrift für Volkskunde*. Nr. II, 279–285.

Heuberger, Valeria & Riegler, Henriette & Vidovic, Hermine (eds.) (1999). *At the Crossroads: Disaster or Normalization. The Yugoslav Successor States in the 1990's*. Frankfurt/M etc.: Lang.

Hujic, Lida (1996). 'I hope you're enjoying your party. MTV in wartorn Bosnia.' *Screen* 37/3, 268–277.

Janjatovic, Petar (1998). *Ilustrovana Yu rock enciklopedija 1960–1997*. Beograd: Geopoetika.

Jez, Boris (1995). *Nikoli vec YU? Bela knjiga o razpadu Jugoslavije*. Ljubljana: Slon.

Mursic Rajko (1995). 'Mnozicna, sodobna kultura na etnoloski nacin.' *Glasnik slovenskega etnoloskega drustva* 35/4, 27–31.

Mursic, Rajko (1999). 'On Globalization, Westernisation, Popular Music and Similar Issues in the Times of the Transition of Post-socialist Countries.' Mursic, Rajko & Brumen, Borut (eds) (1999). *Cultural Processes and Transformations in Transition of the Central and Eastern European Post-communist Countries.* Ljubljana: Etnoloska sticisca, Nr. 9, 139–156.

Pettan, Svanibor (1996). *Balkan Popular Music? No thanks. The View from Croatia.* Unpublished manuscript.

Pettan, Svanibor (ed.) (1998). *Music, Politics and War. Views from Croatia.* Zagreb: Institute of Ethnology and Folklore Research.

Pieper, Werner (ed.) (1999). *Verfemt, verbannt, verboten. Musik & Zensur.* Löhrbach: Der Grüne Zweig.

Povrzanovic, Maja (1983). '"Novokomponirana narodna glasba" – Predmet etnomuzikoloskog istrazivanja?' In: Bogataj, Janez & Terseglav, Marko (eds.). *Zbornik 1. Kongresa jugoslovanskih etnologov in folkloristov.* Ljubljana: Knjiznica Glasnika Slovenskega etnoloskega drustva 10/2, 775–981.

Radio B92: http://www.freeb92.net

Radio zid: http://www.cyvezid.com

Rauhut, Michael (1993). *Beat in der Grauzone. DDR-Rock 1964 bis 1972.* Berlin: Basis Druck.

Reports from the conference 'Balkan Popular Music', which took place from the 22nd to the 24th of November 1996 in Ljubljana. Unpublished manuscripts.

Reuer, B. B. (ed.) (1999). *Musik im Umbruch. Kulturelle Identität und gesellschaftlicher Wandel in Südosteuropa.* Munich: Verlag Süddeutsches Kulturwerk.

Seidel-Pielen, Eberhard (1996). 'Musik statt Granaten. Vier Bands aus dem Berliner Underground auf Tournee durch das Nachkriegs-Bosnien.' www.ds@sonntagsblatt.de, 19. IV.

Slosar, Irina (1997). *Verschwiegenes Serbien. Stimmen für die Zukunft.* Klagenfurt: Wieser.

'Special Focus: Sarajevo' (1991/92). *Balkanmedia,* winter issue, 36–43.

Sundhaussen, Holm (1993). *Experiment Jugoslawien. Von der Staatsgründung bis zum Staatszerfall.* Mannheim, Leipzig, Vienna, Zurich: B. I. Taschenbuch Verlag.

Tomc, Gregor (1998). 'Trdozivi jugorock.' *Delo.* 30. IV, 41.

Tuksar, Stanislav (1978). 'Prisutnost pop und rock glazbe u jugoslovenkom glazbenem zivotu.' *Zvuk.* St. 10. Zagreb. p. 10–13.

Virant, Jana (1998). 'Longplay. Zavrtite si longplay intervju s Saso-Losicem-Loso.' *P. S.* June, 25–29.

Wachtel, Andrew Baruch (1998). *Making a Nation, Breaking a Nation. Literature and Cultural Politics in Yugoslavia.* Stanford: Stanford University Press.

Walker, Tom (2000). 'Bloody king of the mobsters.' *Sunday-Times online,* www.the-times.co.uk. 16. I.

Discography

Bijelo dugme: Pljuni i zapjevaj moja Jugoslavijo. LP, Diskoton, 8244.

Plavi orkestar: Smrt fasizmu. LP, Jugoton, LSV 63262.

Videography

Za slobodu (For the Freedom). Orfej. HRT Zagreb.

7 Globalization – localization, homogenization – diversification and other discordant trends: A challenge to music policy makers[1]

Krister Malm

A policy maker is trying to formulate an action plan within a given legislative and organizational framework in order to direct developments towards a certain desired state or result. A fundamental prerequisite when formulating policies for music and related areas is of course an understanding of processes and relational forces that shape the music scenes. But in a complex world it is very hard to grasp what is going on. The structure of the music industry, the means of disseminating music and the music itself are rapidly transformed. There are different processes of change at hand that seem to be completely discordant. You listen for a pattern but what you hear is cacophony.

Some of these discordant trends are:

- On the one hand more and more homogeneity in music life. The same kind of institutions, media, modes of presentation, etc. can be found all over. On the other there is more and more diversity and multiculturality.
- On the one hand more and more global music styles are being established. On the other local music styles seem to become increasingly important to people.
- On the one hand there are more and more 'hybrid' styles. On the other there is a trend towards preservation and even purification, 'true' and 'authentic' performances, ethnic and other cleansing in music.
- On the one hand there is more and more mediated music. On the other the number of new practitioners of live music in a variety of styles from different times and places is growing day by day.
- On the one hand there is an increasing emphasis on the individual, be it the megastar or the lone walker privately listening to the Walkman. On the other different groupings become more and more visible, groupings using music to mark ethnicity, age, gender and other extra musical bonding, or

even groupings generated by music such as the hip-hop grouping, the rave crowd etc.

- On the one hand the Great Traditions in concert halls, opera houses, festivals, and institutionalized religions etc. seem to become more and more dominant. On the other there is an upsurge of little traditions: didjeridoo playing, djembe drumming and Irish fiddling.

One way to examine and manage these disparities is to use the notion of - *fields of tension*. Between different opposing power sources, flows and valences of different strengths and directions appear. The sources of power and the valences constitute the fields of tension. The enumeration above gives us six interrelated and partly overlapping fields of tension that have become increasingly charged during the last decades.

HOMOGENEOUS – DIVERSE

GLOBAL – LOCAL

HYBRID – PURE

MEDIATED MUSIC – LIVE MUSIC

INDIVIDUAL – COLLECTIVE

THE GREAT TRADITION – THE LITTLE TRADITION

The first two of these fields of tension are of overriding importance to policy making. They extend their influence into all the other fields and are also affected by the other fields. Thus I will concentrate on those in this paper in order to give an idea of how the 'fields of tension' approach can be used in trying to understand a complex reality.

Diversification is a topical subject today. It is easy to reach the conclusion that cultural diversity is growing through migration, through new media channels, etc. But the concurrent homogenization of cultural forms of expression and the extremely powerful monopolization and integration of the world's cultural production into a few transnational giant industrial conglomerates have in recent years been paid less attention. Typical of developments on a world-wide level are not only increasing cultural variation, but the fact that these centrifugal forces are paralleled by ever-stronger centripetal forces: for the first time in history it is beginning to become meaningful to refer, in some respects, to 'the world' in the singular.

The interplay between these important structural opposites, homogenization and diversification, is profoundly affecting the development and production of cultural expressive forms. We have on the one hand an increasing concentration of power and capital – ever-greater global hegemonization –

and on the other hand an increasing diversity and fragmentation of life spheres. If – as a number of cultural researchers suggest – there is a tendency towards increased diversity, a 'symphony of human variations', then it is important to establish the identity of the conductors, composers and producers of this symphony.

There is also, at least in Western countries, an important sub-field of tension close to the diversity pole – a tension between cultural diversity and multiculturality. This sub-field also has strong links to the individual – collective, hybrid – pure and the Great Traditions – little traditions fields. I will try to run down a few properties of the poles of this sub-field.

The concept 'cultural diversity' has its origin in the liberal ideology. Here the individual is in focus. 'Freedom of choice' is the basic goal, the more choice the more freedom for the individual. The motto is 'More is beautiful'. A common metaphor is the botanical garden full of rare plants. But when you look closer, 'more' in praxis doesn't mean more of anything. There are gardeners that keep the weeds out of the garden. The means of getting more is usually deregulation. Society and culture are seen as homogenous. The advocates of diversity aspire to include all realms of reality. Everybody should participate. But at praxis level what is covered is only some realms of reality, mainly the world of high art, the Great Traditions. There is strong gate-keeping by taste police.

The concept of 'multiculture/multicultural' has its origin in Marxist theory linked with an ethnic discourse that emerged around 1970 in the wake of the Black Power movement in the USA. Here the group is in focus. The goal is 'roots rights': visibility, attention and recognition through a collective cultural heritage. The motto is 'Roots are beautiful'. There should be many different groups/'cultures', which in praxis means ethnic groups. A common metaphor is the mosaic. Ethnic activists watch the borders of the squares of this mosaic. There is a strong link to 'folk', 'the little traditions', recently in political discourse turning into 'heritage' with its genetic connotations. Ownership becomes important. In praxis 'heritage' means a limited number of practices in music, dance, food, clothes and certain verbal forms, performed in specific arenas and situations. Emblematic use of specific expressive forms is common. Society and culture are seen as heterogeneous, divided into bounded groupings. There is usually inclusiveness at a societal level, but exclusiveness at group level.

Many cultural politicians and policy makers have locked themselves onto one of these sub-poles or paradigms. Policies based on the cultural diversity concept have not taken the forces of homogenization into account. When deregulating broadcasting in order to get a greater diversity of music output on the radio no attention is paid to the homogenizing force of formatting and streamlining of music content in order to define the audience and sell it to advertisers. Because the USA has not signed the Rome convention on neighbouring rights US records are cheaper to play on European radio stations than those from Europe. The effects of this are not considered. The result is, as we all know, not more of different kinds of music but more of the same. When French authorities wanted to counteract the streamlining forces by prescribing a minimum quota of French music content in TV and radio, they were shocked when this quota was filled with the music of French rappers of immigrant background and not with chanson or other 'appropriate' French music.

The use of policies and resulting strategies based on the multiculturality concept has produced conformity in means. A lot of different groups declare 'We are different!' But they all have to do it in the same ways, with the same means and modes of performance on the same kind of arenas. Forces at work at the homogenization pole have not been taken into account.

Most of the policy makers are not even aware of the sub-poles cultural diversity and multiculturality. Thus there are constant misunderstandings. In the UNESCO report 'Our Cultural Diversity' there are many examples where the authors jump between the poles of cultural diversity and multiculturality even within the same sentence. This produces very unclear and confused conclusions. An analysis that doesn't recognize this sub-field of tension has difficulties in dealing with many current developments where the individual is linked to tradition, or even many different traditions becoming a 'multi-cultural individual'. An illustration here is the incapability of cultural policy makers to deal with senior citizens (seen as individuals since they are not an ethnic group) that like the popular music from the 1940s (not art, not folk). This is a rapidly growing grouping in the Western world but their music is very much absent from public media, clubs, etc. The grouping doesn't belong to any one of the poles but is a product of the tension between the poles. Thus the policy makers do not see it.

Another example is the 'world music' fans, people who like both 'pure' ethnic musics of different kinds and the mixtures of these and global musics, often referred to as 'world beat'. They are in the field of tension between the poles and not at any single pole. Thus the policy makers do not see them. The same could be said of the growing grouping of 'medievalists' in Europe acting out medieval life in carnival-like 'medieval weeks'. In 1998 there were more chivalry tournaments held in Europe than during the full span of the Middle Ages. And probably more medieval music was played than during any single decade during the Middle Ages. The tourist industry has noticed this development, but not the cultural policy makers.

Global – local is a field of tension where one aspect concerns how local forms, styles and genres are picked up and 'mediaized' (adapted to mass media packaging) and via mediation made available regionally, nationally and globally. What can be called 'international communities of interest' are created around, e.g., a global music style. Another aspect concerns how global forms of expression acquire a local meaning and significance – even though a small number of styles, artists and genres have been spread more or less globally they do not have the same meaning, significance and function everywhere.

Of particular importance are the global forms communicating 'multiculture' which allow us to identify, estimate and evaluate the differences between on the one hand the former 'monocultural' and the present 'multicultural', let's say Sweden, and on the other hand 'multicultural Sweden' and other multicultural societies. An extremely interesting special case is that which can be called 'national' from an international point of view – in which global forms attain a distinctive national meaning – and the ways in which immigrants in e.g. Sweden give their native forms of dance and music local 'Swedish' meaning.

An illustration of a common pattern within the global – local field of tension is rap music and hip-hop culture. This pattern is in short: A local music style is, after having moved through migration to a metropolis, picked up by the music industry and distributed globally which results in new local music styles in different places on the globe.

The style later called 'rap' emerged in an African-American context in Jamaica in the 1960s. It was called dub since recorded music was dubbed from a number of shellac records through a primitive mixer unto a new shellac record. This was a form of sampling or African-American *musique concrete* sparked by the same technological innovations that gave birth to electronic music in Europe. The 'dub mix' record was used by the DJ at one of the sound systems (mobile street discos) as background to 'toasting' (from giving a toast speech), that is rhythmical rhymed speech. Jamaican immigrants such as DJ Cool Herc brought this musical praxis to the Bronx in New York City at the end of the 1960s. Here it was turned into rap and combined with break dance, graffiti and other expressions to form hip-hop. Around 1980 the music industry picked up this still fairly local music and started to distribute it. The rest is history.

Young people today practice rap music all over the world. But it has many different local forms and meanings. In Sweden rap in the capital Stockholm is different from rap in Haparanda at the border between Sweden and Finland, in the far north. French rap is different from Greek rap. Rap in East Africa is again a different rap style.

For instance, in Tanzania rap is a fairly new style. Thus what can be perceived as 'homogenization' at a global level is a diversification, the introduction of a new style, at the local Tanzanian level. Rap in Swahili has given the traditionally very silent and subdued youth a voice. All of a sudden through rap in their national language young people have got access to the media. Their rap is molded by the Arabic-African Swahili poetic traditions and the content feeds on post-colonial Tanzanian philosophies. For instance those philosophies exclude 'gangsta' rap and graffiti, and thus they are not part of the Tanzanian hip-hop scene. The musical form and performance style can be close to US models, but also very localized with African instruments and movements from current East African popular dancing.[2]

A pattern that is getting more common is the direct interaction between local and local with very little involvement of the transnational culture industry. Networks of followers of a certain kind of music are formed through migration, traveling, the Internet, etc. These networks can be called 'interlocal communities of interest'.

An example of such a community of interest is the followers of Trinidadian carnival music, soca and steelband, in different parts of the world. In Sweden a group was established in the early 1980s, when West Indian style carnivals were staged in a number of towns and suburbs. During the 1980s steelbands were formed, active interaction with carnival music circles in Trinidad, United Kingdom, USA, Canada and other places started. In the 1990s steel pan teaching and steelband as a student orchestra ventured into municipality music schools in Sweden. On September 20, 1999 the first meeting of representatives of European steelbands was held in Paris with participants from seven countries. At this meeting a European steel-band festival was planned for the year 2000 which will lead up to an international steelband festival in Trinidad and Tobago. The broadcasting media and electronic distribution has meant very little to the development of the interlocal community around Trinidad carnival music. There are still hardly any commercial records featuring steelband music on the market. Narrowcasting (e.g. the Internet) and migration of Trinidadians and other West Indians to Europe are more important factors.

Also in this context local variants emerge. The carnival songs and dance styles practiced at suburban carnivals in Sweden are very different form those in the Trinidad carnival.

The creation of a virtual Assyrian nation on the World Wide Web is another example of an interlocal network created through the Internet.[3] A substantial number of followers of the Syrian Orthodox Church have migrated from the Middle East during the 20th Century. Now around five million live in exile, mainly in the USA, Australia, Germany and Sweden. They have no 'homeland' to return to. Many of these have acquired a secular identity as Assyrians, since they see themselves as the descendants of the inhabitants of the ancient Assyrian Empire. During the past few years activists among these Assyrians have constructed a virtual nation. This Assyrian nation of course has its music, including a national anthem, a history, language courses, children's books, TV and radio stations, etc.: everything that is required to make a nation and all on the Internet. On websites such as 'Nineveh On-line' you can find everything imaginable concerning Assyrian culture. This activity also has its parallels in the real world. An Assyrian soccer team has fought its way right up to the first division of the Swedish soccer league!

When seen as results of opposing forces produced by power sources creating fields of tension, most of the contradicting phenomena touched on above can be comprehended. Instead of looking at the momentary situation within a single kind of music or cultural genre, it is the processes generated by the combined forces of the power sources which must be understood. By making an analysis using the fields-of-tension approach and identifying the processes at work, the policy maker stands a better chance of formulating a valid strategy for manipulation of these power sources and thus directing developments towards desired states or results. It's a great challenge!

Notes

1 This paper is based on interim results of the research project Music – Media – Multiculture <http://www.musakad.se/mmm> carried out by Dan Lundberg, Krister Malm and Owe Ronström at the Royal Swedish Academy of Music, Stockholm. In this paper I try to deal with quite complicated processes in a very condensed way. Thus empirical data to support the statements are not included. Video clips supplemented the originally read paper.

2 More about rap in Nairobi, Dar es Salaam and Lusaka can be found at <http://www. musakad.se/mmm/africa>). Also cf. P. Remes (1999). 'Global Popular Musics and Changing Awareness of Urban Tanzanian Youth.' *Yearbook for Traditional Music*, Vol. 31, 1–26.

3 This process is thoroughly described at the website 'A Virtual Assyria' <http://www. musakad.se/mmm/cyberland>.

8 Music policy between safeguarding and chauvinism

Alfred Smudits

The relationship between global and local music

Transnational music corporations are increasingly owned by an alliance of Japanese, European and US-American interests, but it is becoming more and more difficult to locate the source of 'their' culture.[1] Global popular music, or transnational music does not correspond to 'Anglo-American' popular music per se. There are economic forces that influence the strategies of global entertainment corporations in order to promote international acts, but at the same time to take care of local markets with specific demands.

This partly contradictory situation seems to bring out more and more a symbiotic relationship between global corporations and local musics. Global corporations are acting rather conservatively by developing and promoting new sounds and genres. It is much easier to promote well accepted international sounds than to develop new and risky ones. From an economic point of view it is rational. But sometimes (and maybe more and more often) the demand for something 'new' can not be ignored and has to be satisfied. The transnational mainstream always needs some salt or new blood to be attractive again and again. This new blood comes from the local musics as the experience of the whole history of popular music teaches us: the inputs to the transnational mainstream coming from Bossa Nova, Tango, Reggae, Salsa, Rai, Rap, Grunge, Techno, etc. were not invented by the global corporations; they originated from local musics beyond the industrialized music business.

So: global corporations need local musics, but do local musics need global corporations? Under the circumstances of the world economy we are witnessing now, the answer is clearly yes. All other options would be romantic. Local musics need the infrastructures of the music industries to be heard throughout the world and very often even to be heard on the local level. The question that is not answered yet is that of the balance of power between global corporations and local musics. Because the danger of being exploited and expropriated still exists for local musics, they are distributed worldwide but do not receive the revenue which they should. At this stage the relationship between global industries and local musics would be a parasitic rather than a symbiotic one.

The second problem is that local music needs a minimum of infrastructure to be able to develop sufficiently to reach the global market. At the moment this still should be the task of national music politics.

Such policies[2] can aim at mainly financial support of local music development or the support of national music industries so that they can enter the world market more easily.

Other responding strategies could be efforts to improve the legal framework for music production and especially distribution in favour of local artists. Examples which already existed in several countries are:

- The use of the revenue of levies on empty tapes
- Quotas favouring the amount of domestic music in the airplay of radio stations
- Taxes on sound carriers
- A public domain, i. e. a levy for the use of unprotected music (folk or classical), etc.

Whether such policy measures are aimed at the safeguarding of authentic indigenous musics or the strengthening of the infrastructures of a local musical life, they are confronted with one crucial problem: the definition of what is to be understood by 'local', 'domestic', 'national' and 'indigenous'.

Definitions of 'domestic' music

In several countries regulations to define a minimum share of domestic music in radio programs (quotas) are being discussed; in international statistics of the phonographic industry a category called 'domestic share' can be found; the European music industry is celebrating the constantly growing amounts of European music in the total turnover of sound carriers of the nineties.

But what does 'domestic music' mean, which criteria have to be fulfilled so a piece of music can be identified with a country, a specific region? And who defines these criteria?

Usually it seems that a mixture of several criteria are used when music is classified as domestic:[3] the nationality of the composer, the author of the lyrics, the singer or instrumentalist; place of production; the language of the lyrics; the aesthetic association of a specific genre or style with a specific region or nation (Viennese waltz, Italian opera, Chicago blues, etc.)

When discussing the problem of domestic music seriously, there are two possibilities, a more sophisticated, culturalistic approach and a more pragmatic, sociological one:

Dealing with the problem from a culturalistic point of view will always lead to a deconstruction of the category 'domestic'. No serious musicological or musical criteria can be found which will define a piece of music essentially as domestic. 'Domesticness' will always be an ideological category, with no empirical backbone but the people who believe (but cannot prove objectively) that a piece of music is domestic. (Compare the discussion of the terms: nation, nation-state, cultural identity, or the discussions about citizenship for immigrants.[4])

What is 'domestic' for one group (e.g. because they are speaking for the national composers' society, and therefore only accept citizenship of the composer as a legal criterion) is 'foreign' for other groups (e.g. because every kind of pop music is Anglo-American to them). This shows that from different points of view different criteria are used and therefore each definition of 'domestic music' will be arbitrary in the last consequence.

Even a very sophisticated aesthetic analysis would have to come to the conclusion that a 'point zero' does not exist for any musical tradition (where 'domesticness' could perhaps be fixed), because every musical tradition has developed out of other preceding musical traditions.[5] (There might be one special case namely that of so-called autochthonous folk music. Here a specific musical style can be associated with a specific geographic region – but this is true only as long as this music is not 'discovered' by the rest of the world – which might be the next valley.)

From a pragmatic, more sociological point of view there is the possibility of pure stocktaking of existing efforts to define 'domesticness'. Each definition is of course the result of a specific group's interests, corresponding with its very specific economic, political or ideological position.

For example, in the case of radio quotas: composers will try to improve the amount of broadcasted music composed by domestic composers, regardless of how this music sounds; 'guardians of language' will try to define 'domesticness' via the language used; 'guardians of cultural values' will argue in the same way as composers' organizations but narrow their definition towards music of high quality, etc.

The relationship between both of the possibilities for analyzing 'domesticness' is complementary. In both cases the result for those who expect an essential solution of the problem of 'domesticness' will be dissatisfying.

The solution from a deconstructional point of view will of course be very correct from an ethic point of view: 'domesticness' as an ideological position, usually used to disguise political or economic interests.

But how does knowing this help those involved with music policy, as a great deal of it is based on definitions of 'domesticness', whether they make sense or not objectively.

So what can we do, that is useful? Stocktaking does in fact make sense, even as only a part of the strategy of deconstruction. Here the material has to be systematically prepared and can be deconstructed later on. The different positions taken for defining 'domesticness' are ideological positions in disguise, sometimes very clever disguise, sometimes very poor. But to make the ideological character of these definitions evident is very important work, maybe a good precondition for self-assured (but of course no guarantee for successful) political action in this field.

If one takes a very concrete look at the different definitions of 'domesticness' the following categorization might be useful:

1. *'Significantly vague'* A lot of definitions can be identified which can be classified as being 'significantly vague'. Within them the following formulations are used: 'compositions of domestic origin', of 'national origin'; 'national composers'; the 'share of domestic music'; the 'consideration of domestic originators/authors'. Sometimes a concrete nationality is used for 'national' or 'domestic': 'Austrian', 'British', 'French', but also 'European'. Sometimes only the 'consideration of domestic culture', or of 'regional, local or national cultural specifics', 'of contemporary works of art' or 'cultural creation' is demanded.

Principally three different approaches can be distinguished:

- An author-oriented approach (possible indicator: citizenship, place of birth, where s/he pays taxes, etc.)
- An 'opus'-oriented approach (possible indicator: national collecting society)
- A production-oriented approach (possible indicators: publisher, phonographic industry, place of signing).

But all definitions are vague insofar as there are no indicators, no specifications given concerning what 'domestic', 'national', etc. means. One can suppose that this has some good reasons: to decide concretely what is meant by those vague terms has to be, and of course will be, negotiated between different interest groups. Vagueness guarantees flexibility and therefore vagueness is significant for these specific kinds of definitions of 'domesticness'.

They are ethically motivated recommendations, and concretization is the object of negotiations.

2. *A partial concretization* It is the case, when 'domesticness' is defined by the language used (which only works with vocal music?!). The actual regulation of radio quotas in France is a good example for this (40% of the broadcasted music has to be of French origin): French rock bands singing in English or Rai artists singing in Northern African dialects are not counted toward the quota, although the artists are French citizens.

Partial concretization is characterized by a one-dimensional definition, which can be examined very clearly – no negotiations are necessary or possible.

The motivation for this kind of regulation is obviously a very strange mix of economic and cultural reasons.

3. *The integration of complexity* An approach aiming at the integration of complexity, that means integration of the numerous factors which might be used to describe 'domesticness', which at the same time attempts to guarantee the possibility of formal examination, is demonstrated by the Canadian case. There are four criteria two of which have to be fulfilled for definition as Canadian content. They are: composer is Canadian, lyricist is Canadian, main singer/musician is Canadian, place of production is in Canada.

There is of course still the problem of defining 'Canadian' in relation to individuals (see above) but what is essential is that there is a totally different motivation as compared to the significant vagueness described above. The Canadian attempt is not only ethically motivated but also aims at a practical application.

4. *Cultural and aesthetic criteria* Interesting enough to be mentioned is the fact that no regulatory effort can be identified which only argues with cultural and aesthetic criteria. To define 'domesticness' via aesthetic traditions or something similar seems to be too dangerous to be stressed in the context of music policy.

Conclusion

When discussing the 'domesticness' of music the task for scientific work is twofold:
- To criticize essential definitions as ideological concepts and study their ideological motivations (who is interested in defining a specific kind of music as domestic – and why) and
- In spite of that still strive for the elaboration of pragmatic and formally examinable concepts of 'domesticness', partly to develop valid and reliable indicators, partly to offer concepts for music-policy makers.

Notes

1 Several scholars have worked on that issue, some of them have contributed to this very publication. For my own position (Bontinck/Smudits 1997, Smudits 1998) the following publications have been of importance: Burnett 1996, european music office 1996, Garofalo 1993, ifpi 1996, Larkey 1993, Laing 1986, Malm/Wallis 1992, Mitchell 1996, Negus 1994, Regev 1997, Rutten 1991.
2 A discussion of concrete measures in different countries can be found in MEDIACULT (1990) or Negus (1994).
3 The following examples are taken from several journals such as *Österreichische Autorenzeitung, Coda, music and media*, and especially from Shaughnessy/Fuente Cobo (1990), MEDIACULT (1990) and Ottawa (2000). A more detailed mode of reference seemed to be too complicated for the purposes of the this article.
4 Compare amongst many others Donald & Rattansai 1992 or Rajchman 1995.
5 It was especially Ed Larkey who convinced me – in long discussions – that this is true.

References

Bontinck, Irmgard and Alfred Smudits (1997). *Music and Globalization*. Final Report prepared for the Annual Report of the World Culture and Development of UNESCO. Vienna.

Burnett, Robert (1996). *The Global Jukebox. The International Music Industry.* London/New York: Routledge.

Donald, James and Ali Rattansi, Ali (eds.) (1992). *'Race', Culture, and Difference.* London: Sage.

European Music Office (ed.) (1996). *Music in Europe.* A study carried out by the European Music Office with the support of the European Commission (DGX).

Garofalo, Reebee (1993). 'Whose World, What Beat: The Transnational Music Industry, Identity, and Cultural Imperialism.' *The world of music* 35(2), 16–32.

IFPI (1996). *The Recording Industry in Numbers '96.* London: IFPI.

Laing, Dave (1986). 'The music industry and the "cultural imperialism" thesis.' *Media, Culture & Society* Vol. 8, No. 3, 331–341.

Larkey, Edward (1993). *Pungent Sounds. Constructing Identity with Popular Music in Austria.* New York: Peter Lang.

Malm, Krister and Wallis, Roger (1992). *Media Policy and Music Activity.* London: Routledge.

MEDIACULT (1990). *The role of communication technologies in the safeguarding and enhancing of European unity and cultural diversity.* Part I: Proposals. Study undertaken at the request of the Council of Europe. Vienna.

Mitchell, Tony (1996). *Popular Music and Local Identity. Rock, Pop and Rap in Europe and Oceania.* London/New York: Leicester University Press.

Negus, Keith (1994). 'Transnational Policies and Local Predicaments. The Recording Industry and the (Re)Construction of European Musical Identities.' In: Ales Opekar (ed.). *Central European Popular Music*, Prague: Czech branch of Iaspm, 7–11.

Ottawa, Ulrike (2000). *Oesterreichische Popmusik und OE3. Ein gestörtes Verhältnis?* Vienna: Institut für Musiksoziologie.

Rajchman, John (ed.) (1995). *The Identity in Question.* London: Routledge.

Regev, Matti (1997). 'Rock Aesthetics and Musics of the World.' *Theory, Culture and Society*, Vol. 14 (3), 125–142.

Rutten, Paul (1991): 'Local popular music on the national and international markets.' *Cultural Studies* Vol. 5, No. 3, 294–305.

Shaughnessy, Haydn/Fuente Cobo, Carmen (1990). *The Cultural Obligations of Broadcasting.* (Media Monograph No. 12). Manchester: The European Institute for the Media, Council of Europe.

Smudits, Alfred (1998). 'Musik und Globalisierung. Die phonographischen Industrien. Strukturen und Strategien.' *Österreichische Zeitschrift für Soziologie*, Vol. 23, No. 2, 23–52.

Journals

Coda – Zeitschrift der Musikergilde, Vienna, several volumes since 1995.

Music and media, London, several volumes since 1997.

Österreichische Autorenzeitung, (edited by AKM – Society of Authors, Composers and Music Publishers Limited), Vienna, several volumes since 1975.

Part III:
Approaches and methods:
Popular music research between
'production of culture' and
'anthropology'

9 Up and down the music world. An anthropology of globalization

Joana Breidenbach and Ina Zukrigl

New Year celebrations in Japan aren't a success without the performance of Beethoven's *Ninth Symphony*. For the New Year festivities the national TV station transmits not only the performance of the symphony but also the many auditions of amateur choirs rehearsing the pronunciation of Schiller's lyrics *Ode an die Freude*. The symphony was introduced in 1918 when German prisoners of war performed it in the city of Naruto to show their gratitude for the good treatment they received from their captors. The highly impressed citizens declared the first Sunday in June as the day of the *Ninth Symphony*. Today, for many Japanese the symphony is a symbol of understanding and friendship. According to a leading critic it even presents a new form of the Shintoist cleansing ritual *misogi*. When Japanese record companies set the time standard for CD production in the 1970s, they used the duration of Beethoven's most famous piece.

At the beginning of the 21st century we encounter the familiar in unexpected places. The boundaries between skin colours, geographical places, languages and lifestyles are blurring. How can we come to terms with the changing realities all over the world?

The ethnographic method

Cultural and social anthropology, in the German-speaking world also known as *Ethnologie*, is, loosely defined, devoted to the study of the 'man-made part of environment', to human existence in all its diversity. Historically, anthropologists studied the social and cultural organization of non-Western societies. But in recent years this artificial dichotomy between the modern West and the traditional rest has been questioned and largely overcome. Today anthropologists study African kinship and management techniques, conflict resolution in Mexico as well as in Germany, the uses of the Internet in Trinidad and Great Britain. Whereas 20 years ago most anthropologists concentrated on small-scale societies in rural settings, like villages or bands of hunters and gatherers, this has changed radically too, as more and more anthropologists study either 'at home', in urban settings or realize that, given the increasing global interconnections between far-away spaces, different locations have to be studied in order to reach a satisfactory analysis of social and cultural phenomena.

Good anthropology combines detailed empirical research with larger political and philosophical questions. Anthropologists do 'participant observation'. This research method involves going 'into the field' for an extended period of time (generally 12–18 months) and living the life of the group studied. During fieldwork, anthropologists collect data by using a whole range of qualitative and quantitative methods (observation, natural conversation, various kinds of interviews, checklists, questionnaires as well as unobtrusive methods, such as behavior trace studies or archival research). The toolbox of an anthropologist can be very large and generally the questions will drive the methods employed.

Participant observation involves establishing rapport in a new community, blending in the local scene as much as possible, so that people go about their business as usual. This makes it possible to collect data normally not easily open to analysis and reduces the problem of reactivity.

A number of prominent characteristics distinguishes the anthropological and ethnographic approach from other social and cultural sciences (although in the past decade a number of disciplines have incorporated participant observation into their own approaches).

The emic perspective

During fieldwork the anthropologist attempts to take the perspective of the people he/she is studying. In the words of Malinowski, the goal of ethnography is 'to grasp the native's point of view, his relation to life, to realize his visions of his world'. This so-called emic perspective represents a fundamental check on the general assumptions of the researcher. While other social sciences and the general public discourse normally generalize from their own (in our case Western) point of view, anthropologists, by their training, are encouraged to take nothing for granted, and expect the unexpected. This way, they often come forward with counterintuitive evidence. When looking at the cultural consequences of globalization, anthropologists question the prominent Western scenarios (homogenization, fragmentation) and look closer at the *meanings* different people attribute to globally available goods, media, ideas and institutions. By asking questions like, how do Arabs interpret Dallas, what do Pakistani generals mean when talking about human rights, why is Beethoven so popular in Japan, anthropologists are taking the perspective of the cultural insider and represent and translate their findings to a wider audience (most often outsiders to the cultural scene under observation).

Here is one example for the emic perspective. In the early 1990s young British Asians, the sons and daughters of immigrants from the Punjab and East Africa living in the London district of Southall, were avid fans of the Australian TV soap Neighbours. Everyday talk among teenagers was filled with references to the series' characters and for outsiders it was often difficult to distinguish whether the names mentioned in discussions belonged to real friends or the actors of the fictional Ramsey Street. On first sight this was yet another example of the westernization and homogenization of teenagers globally, and many parents of the young Asians certainly viewed series like Neighbours as a fundamental threat to their own values and cultural identity. But why exactly was the series so popular? In the ethnographic analysis by Marie Gillespie (1995) it turns out, that the Asian teenagers didn't find the Australian living conditions per se very attractive, nor did they try to copy the series characters. But they did see very strong similarities between their own social worlds and the ones depicted in Neighbours. In both, there existed very dense social networks which exerted a high degree of social control especially over teenage girls. Gossip and rumours prevailed and mothers and aunts constantly monitored and regulated their behavior. This social control was perceived as a heavy burden by the teenagers, who were searching for their own identity as British Asians and who didn't want to emulate their parents' way of life uncritically. In Neighbours they saw how their fictional Australian peers coped with social and parental authority. Their own cultural sense of appropriateness and family honour often forbade the Asian teenagers to talk about certain topics, like violence in the family or romantic relations, freely with their friends. Instead they used Neighbours as a screen which allowed them to talk indirectly about sensitive issues of importance to them. In this way they explored and found values and forms of expression which were compatible with their own cultural and religious background as well as with their lives in Great Britain.

The holistic approach

On a research spectrum ranging from ecological to laboratory methods, participant observation leans far to the ecological pole. Scientists working within the laboratory model focus on the specialization of methods and the control over variables. Anthropologists on the other hand favour an open research approach which aims at a holistic vision of the society in question. It tries to overcome the artificial separation of analytical categories (such as politics, culture and economy). A single phenomenon is studied in its social context, and the interpenetration of different aspects of human life, of, let's say, legal practices, gender relations, rituals and social structure is of central concern. During fieldwork anthropologists come to understand one phenomenon as an idiom for something else and see the interconnections between highly diverse aspects of life.

The American medical anthropologist Emily Martin (1994) started her research on historically changing health paradigms and the different visions of health and illness held by various strata of society. She studied members of the medical profession and the work in laboratories, different social groups in the town of Baltimore as well as AIDS activists and hospice volunteers. The focus of the study was how scientific knowledge moves in and out the laboratory on to the streets and how it changes thereby. While in the first part of this century illness was predominantly explained by insufficient protection against the *entry* of viruses and bacteria into the body, since the 1970s the battle between health and illness has been conceptualized as a fight *inside* the body with the immune system acting as the major guardian of health. The governing paradigm for a functioning immune system turned out to be flexibility. But flexibility (originating from systems theory) is not only the key-term in immunology, but also in a political economic organization. The discourse and practices of flexible specialization, the flexible workforce, etc. dominate the latest economic textbooks and feature prominently in management trainings and economic courses. The resulting ethnography is a book about the development of a general ideology concerning 'flexibility' in an variety of domains (immunology, economics, New Age philosophies, government organizations, psychology, feminism) which appear at first sight unrelated, but which feed off one another, reinforcing the paradigm in a broad range of life.

A comparative perspective

A lot of anthropological research is comparative, either explicitly by comparing two or more social scenes with one another, or implicitly by using the insights gained from the study of a particular study site to other localities. The discipline itself was right from the beginning geared towards an (explicit or implicit) comparison between indigenous lifeworlds and the Western world. The books and films by Margaret Mead, the great popularizer of American cultural anthropology, for example, compare child-rearing techniques, gender relations and the behavior of adolescents in different Pacific societies and the US. Comparison also turned out to be a useful tool for the deconstruction of apparently universal terms and concepts, like religion, consumption, or motherhood.

While attending feminist conferences in the US, the American anthropologist Laura Nader (1990) noticed that the debates between Western and Islamic feminists got into deadlock when both sides accused the other of submitting to their respective patriarchies. In both, East and West, the unit of analysis in feminist studies was a particular society and female subordination was explained by intra-societal factors. Nader decided to conduct a comparative study of gender relations in Western countries and the Middle East. She discovered that in both regions the situation of women in the other region was presented as highly problematic and instrumentalized to justify the existing inequalities in their own countries. Islamic media portray Western women as subordinate and sexual objects. To prove this, they just need to refer to the high rape rate, the multimillion-dollar porno industry or the absence of respect for women as indicated by unequal pay structures. Western industrialized nations are depicted as immoral societies which place their elderly in old peoples' homes and in which women are the main victims of poverty and abuse. In contrast Westerners perceive Moslem females as totally oppressed – they highlight practices such as forced marriage, veiling, polygamy, female circumcision and the general exclusion of women from public life.

By comparing two different patriarchal systems, the anthropologist was able to illustrate how the power relations between two world regions were used to legitimize and perpetuate the subjugation of women in both societies. In both world regions the inside culture is idealized in comparison to the outside culture. This cultural comparison allows members of both East and West to feel superior to each other and control the place of women in society at the same time. In the West as well as in Islamic countries women are pacified by the slogan 'compared to those other women you are well off'.

A vertical slice

Amongst anthropologists it used to be common to study small-scale communities in the Third World or marginalized groups within Western societies. There are far more studies about the Yanomami than about Wall Street law firms. Recently though many anthropologists have broadened the scope of their analysis to include various strata of society, from the local to the global level. A number of anthropologists have succeeded in taking a vertical slice of the phenomena studied and followed their subjects trajectories up and down society. This way far-reaching power relations, hegemonic and counter-hegemonic influences can be made transparent, aspects that get lost when studies are extremely localized or when you try to squeeze the unique into the narrow definitions of scientific variables.

When anthropologist Patricia Marquez (1999) studied the lives of street children in Venezuela, she followed the larger trajectory of street children at various levels. This included not only sharing the tough life with the children on the streets, but also studying family life in the slums of Caracas and the effect of hegemonic notions of what a 'proper' family should be like. Marquez also zooms in on the legal aspects of crime on the street and the consequences of legal categorizations for street children. The analysis finally exposed the corruption and hidden violence permeating the whole social system right up to the ruling classes, as well as the impact of global consumerism on the desires and practices of youngsters.

A check on verbal statements

Research into different methodologies has shown that up to 70% of all verbal statements don't correspond to the observable facts. Participant observation enables the researcher to check verbal statements against concrete behavior.

The British anthropologist Daniel Miller (1989) did a study of everyday shopping in a London street. When handing out questionnaires, he noticed that people tended to confirm the dominant stereotypes about shopping. They described it as superficial, but pleasurable and fun. When studying attitudes towards shopping in focus groups, different aspects of the shopping experience were stressed. People drew attention to the problem of shopping with small children (begging for sweets and making scenes at the counter, where sweets are prominently displayed). When following people up and down the supermarket aisles as part of the participant observation, the reality of shopping turned out to be a far cry from the dominant stereotypes. Shoppers for daily provisions were always in a rush, comparing prices and trying to save money. They were eager to find those products which the family liked, but which were also considered valuable, healthy and educational by the shopper her-/himself. In short: shopping is experienced more as a daily struggle than a hedonistic pastime.

Limitations of the ethnographic method

A brief note on the limitations of the ethnographic method seems in place. Obviously participant observation is a time-consuming and therefore expensive research method. But more serious are the allegations that ethnography is such a subjective research method that it is unscientific. The subjective nature of the ethnographic enterprise received great attention in the 1980s, especially through the work of a number of American cultural anthropologists. Ethnographic fieldwork was now portrayed as being closer to art and literature than science. Obviously, the personality of the fieldworker is of far greater importance than in most other methods. In order to judge ethnographic descriptions and confirm the validity of its findings it is important to know about the specific situation of the research. The influence on research conditions as well as the personality of the fieldworker can be grasped when looking at different ethnographies about the same place (Redfield 1930, Lewis 1951). Possibilities of highlighting and checking the influence of ethnographers on their research are repeated studies or teamwork. Nevertheless, in ethnographic fieldwork it is impossible to get rid of the subjective bias and influences. Findings are 'objective' only in relation to specific circumstances. Many contemporary anthropologists have transformed this self-reflexivity into an asset: a far greater awareness of the limitations of all truth-claims without giving up on them.

Four hypotheses concerning the globalization of culture

What insights does a cultural perspective offer for an understanding of changes in the music world brought about by globalization? Looking at the anthropological record a number of hypotheses concerning the cultural aspects of the current phase of globalization emerge.

People interpret global goods, ideas and concepts in various ways

Goods, ideas and melodies of foreign origin have become part of our lives and routines. Almost on a daily basis people have to decide what to do with foreign influences. Societies don't passively give in to foreign and global influences, but use various strategies for dealing with new cultural imports. In resisting global influences the state is still the most prominent agent. Leading the worldwide battle against Americanization, France in 1996 introduced a national music quota of 40% to protect its national music industry and due to European pressure, the national quota system in the arts survived the liberalization policies passed by the Uruguay Round. But resistance is just one way of dealing with foreign influences. A far more common strategy is to appropriate and integrate them into one's own culture. Anthropological research has stressed the ability of societies to incorporate what might be expected to threaten them. In the process of adopting new influences they are transformed or acquire new symbolic meanings which suit the needs of the given society. As the American anthropologist Marshall Sahlins noted, people use foreign influences 'to become more like themselves' (Sahlins 1987: LXXIV).

Appropriation is an everyday strategy in the music world, ranging from the translation of lyrics to the mixing of whole music traditions. Kenyan Mau Mau rebels took Christian hymns and rewrote the lyrics, 'transforming celestial battles into local ones' (Taylor 1997: 72). Today the mixing and borrowing of tonalities, harmonies and instruments increasingly has a transnational dimension. In Nigeria Fují music has a large following (Barber and Waterman 1995). The most successful bands sell 100,000–200,000 (legal) copies of their records, perform daily on Nigerian television and play at weddings, funerals and other social highlights. Fují developed from *ajisáàri*, the chants used to call for prayer during Ramadan. Two former *ajisáàri* singers, Alhadji Dr. Sikuru Ayinde Barrister and Alhadje Professor Ayinla Kollington, are the superstars of the Fují scene today. The lyrics are a mix of Yoruba and English: 'Don't doubt my love, my sweetie. I love you' is followed by Muslim prayers and Yoruba praise poetry called *oríkì*. The songs are usually about a prominent local or national personality or celebrate the bandleader himself as a pious Muslim, Yoruba praise the singer and successful entrepreneur.

On first hearing, Fují sounds like a plain copy of various Western styles. Fují bands use imported music technology and borrow from Western music traditions. In their videos, transnational status symbols feature prominently:

chic hotel lobbies, fast cars and Western fashion juxtaposed with images of Nelson Mandela. But making a facile distinction between the indigenous and the imported is a mistake. Rather than expressing a postmodern aesthetic, the highly eclectic style is typical for traditional Yoruba praise poetry. Fují just intensifies this well-known performance style. And in keeping with typical Yoruba public performances, the recorded songs are arranged in an uninterrupted continuum, ignoring the 3–5 minute production units of the international music industry.

The popularity of Fují depends on its ability to take its listeners on an imaginative journey across time and space. Through the eclectic mix of lyrics, instruments, music styles and visual clues, various alternative (transnational) lives are evoked. The foreign and the indigenous form an inseparable whole, expressing something truly Nigerian.

Authenticity is a highly contested value and is not based on origins

Though appropriation happens everyday, its evaluation is contested. When the Japanese pianist Mitsuko Uchida plays Mozart, Western critics accept the performance as authentic. But who takes the Korean winner of the world yodelling competition serious? Western classical music is considered universal, whereas folk music performed by a foreigner is perceived as inauthentic. The new category of world music is smiled at by some critics while its listeners and the producers often display an 'anything goes' attitude. Why are some cultural expressions accepted as authentic and others not?

The search for authenticity in the social and material world, as well as concerning the person (in psychoanalysis) began at the end of the last century, at a time when the citizens of the newly industrialized countries had an unprecedented variety of goods, lifestyles and artistic expressions at their disposal. This new range of choice in combination with a disrupted social order, demanded an active positioning of the self. Authenticity came to be an orientation device and a mark of distinction. Until today, authenticity, projected onto objects, tells us something about the person who surrounds him-/herself with these goods. Authenticity is an effective gate-keeping concept. The question is therefore always 'whose authenticity' are we talking about?

According to the popular Western understanding authenticity is based on origins. Something is authentic when we can trace its historical roots. But roots are relative. Pasta is perceived as original Italian cuisine, although noodles were originally imported from China. In globality historical roots become just one criteria for authenticity amongst many others. An import can be authentic as long as it is successfully appropriated by a society. The resulting new cultural forms then express new social realities and cultural identities.

In Southall, the multi-ethnic suburb of London introduced earlier, a number of new authentic lifestyles have emerged, mirroring the mix of highly diverse cultural influences. The streets of Southall are full of Punjabi, Gujarati, Urdu and accents from a number of English-speaking countries. People not only define themselves according to their ethnic or religious background but also call themselves black, feminist or socialist. The various identities vary according to time and context. Many sons and daughters of South Asian immigrants refuse being stereotyped as Sikh or Hindu, categories that, in their view, belong to their parent generation. Like other youngsters they are trying to find a lifestyle of their own that differs from the dominant youth culture in Southall with its symbols borrowed from US street culture. In the newly emerging British Asian youth culture, the reinvention of Bhangra, traditional Punjabi folk music, played an important part. From the late 1970s on Bhangra was performed by live bands in London, who played it with electronic keyboards and guitars, using new sampling and scratching techniques. Originally called *Southall Beat*, Bhangra is performed today by many local bands. Apache Indian, a young British-born musician of Punjabi descent, has achieved stardom not only in Great Britain, but also in India and among Indian communities worldwide. Apache combines Bhangra with Jamaican reggae and raps to the beat of Indian percussion instruments like the *dhol* or the *tabla*. The songs deal with typical problems of young Asian teenagers in Great Britain. 'Arranged Marriage' (1993) describes the dilemma of Asian youth to find their own way between the tradition of arranged marriage and Western conceptions of romantic love:

> (. . .) Now me done get marry but me start to worry,
> Me have to tell you something mom would you help me,
> About me arrange marriage me have a problem,
> When is the right time to tell me girlfriend,
> Beca the time has come mon fe Apache,
> Fe find one gal and get marry, (. . .)

Bangramuffin, as Apache's music is called, is seized by Southall teenagers as a space to mould a new identity. This identity is not necessarily a rejection of their parents' cultural values. In contrast, many young people for example continue to have arranged marriages. But ethnic origins are just one source of identification amongst others. In an interview Apache explains:

We were discouraged from talking about things like sex or contraception or arranged marriages. The new generation of Asian kids wanted to talk about these things and we wanted a street culture of our own. (. . .) The new generation of Asian kids have a new culture that consists of a lot of different things – an Asian thing, a white thing and a black thing. The Asian thing is still very important to them, but I want to put all these things together to take our culture forward (quoted in Taylor 1997: 157).

Global cultural flows break open existing center-periphery relationships

With an increasing access to foreign ideas and goods, the old patterns of centre/periphery relations are changing. In a number of realms the hegemony of the advanced industrial countries is declining. Centers and peripheries are still discernible, but for various areas like technologies, youth cultures or fashion, new centers have emerged. For many, India is a center for spiritual growth and Japan serves as a role model for other Asian countries which emulate it and its ability to selectively adopt foreign ideas and economic practices. China has become a new powerful capitalist center, forging its own vision of modernity.

In globality we witness a disjuncture between the centers for production, mediation and consumption. For many world music artists their home countries are the main source for artistic inspirations, whereas the production equipment, capital, and distributive capacities are located in the West. The fan community is spread throughout the world. As musical traditions are appropriated in different parts of the world, their origins get blurred.

The song 'Malaika', said to be composed by the Kenyan musician Fadhili William, was collected and copyrighted by Pete Seeger while on travel in West Africa in 1963. Later it was covered by Miriam Makeba and Harry Belafonte amongst others under the label of Urban Folk Revival. The Swedish band Hep Stars (later Abba) recorded another version in 1968, and the Germany-based Boney M. covered it from Abba in 1981. It was this latest version that found its way back to Africa and became a national hit in Nigeria when adopted and sung by Fují star Barrister (Barber and Waterman 1995: 274). Meanwhile 17 composers have been mentioned as composers of 'Malaika' (Krister Malm, personal communication).

When looking at recent developments and discourses concerning copyright and patent law, we witness how old power relations are challenged by people from the periphery. Until recently Western musicians freely appropriated musical traditions from all over the world without taking differing notions of ownership into consideration.

The notion of collective ownership held by many indigenous societies stands in sharp contrast to the dominant legal conception of intellectual ownership as an individual right. The Suya Indians of Brazil for example distinguish between individual and collective songs. Collective songs, usually originating from a mythical past, belong to specific social groups. These groups can decide whether the song can be performed by another group. The rights concerning individual songs are more complex. These songs were passed from their originator, usually a plant or a fish, to a human communicator (the composer in Western terminology). The actual owner *(kandé)*, however, is the first person to learn and perform the song. After the death of the owner another performer can acquire the song rights. Who would collect the royalties if 'The Big Turtle Song' became a national chart breaker? The Suya case is even more complicated as under Brazilian law, the Suya are considered minors (Seeger 1997).

Challenges against the individual ownership concept as the basis for all copyright and patent laws have been brought up since the 1970s when countries of the First World started to demand the protection of their cultural heritage and published various declarations and statements on indigenous intellectual property rights. This recent development is part of a growing cultural and political self-confidence of marginalized groups worldwide. The demands of indigenous peoples are discussed in a number of national and international forums. The UNESCO, for example, has come up with the idea of indigenous cultural protection boards that would register the works and authorize their use, allowing exceptions for educational and inspirational purposes (Brown 1998: 203f).

Protection renders ambivalent results: who speaks for a group? What is part of human heritage and what should be protected by law? We might be happy to grant many rights to the Hopi or Yanomami which we wouldn't want to grant to the Catholic Church or Church of Scientology. And how do we reconcile protection of intellectual property with the democratic ideal of the free flow of information? Imagine every artist having to ask the Vatican for permission in order to use the image of the Virgin Mary in his/her painting.

With changes in the old centre-periphery pattern, power relations have become more difficult to detect. When multinational music companies meet transnational artists it's not easy to pin down who gains financially and symbolically from the relationship. Take the case of an African artist under contract with an American label. In statistics on the global music industry, this artist would count as an American artist. According to the same logic Tina Turner raises German national sales figures.

Research about the globalization of music is a complex task requiring us to look at structural as well as symbolic aspects. Analyzing the decision-making processes of the global music industry will tell us something about the way local branches depend on their global company headquarters, but can't explain why Latino music sells very well despite being ignored by the major labels. In order to understand audience preferences we need to study music consumption and the socio-cultural meanings of certain songs and music styles, instead of relying on the dry sales figures of music labels.

The emerging global culture is a hegemony of structure but leads to a pluralization of content

One of the new features of the present period of globalization is the emergence of a global culture consisting of ideas, concepts and goods available to an increasing number of people all over the world. Issues like human rights, the fall of the Berlin Wall or the death of Lady Diana are proliferated through the media and millions of people on the move, like refugees, tourists and businessmen. More and more people reflect their own way of life in the mirror of other ways of life and develop a comparative consciousness.

Global culture refers to a set of common structures and categories that organize difference. While different cultures continue to be quite distinct and varied, they are becoming different in uniform ways. The anthropologist Richard Wilk calls this reference system *structures of common difference*. The term refers to a new global hegemony, which is a hegemony of structure, not of content. Most of the global categories and standards circulating today originate in the West and the West makes a sustained effort to assure their survival, but they also spread because people elsewhere appropriate them. In the process, the hegemonic structures themselves are transformed.

The global music market follows a *structure of common difference*. The criteria which determine success and failure of musicians are largely defined by a handful of big record companies. They create categories like Folk Music, World Music or Indigenous Music into which the immense variety of globally available music styles is forced. Musicians themselves have little influence over their categorization. Affluent Western consumers also largely determine the criteria for authenticity and quality. In order to gain recognition and compete on the world market, musicians are forced to adapt their product to the established categories and expectations. Zairean singer Papa Wemba is explicit about this: 'My original group is there for my Zairean fans who come to hear typical African sounds, but when I decided to be a singer with an international name I formed another group to appeal to a different public, I have never mixed the two since both of them represent different aspects of my musical personality. I believe they should remain separate because I am a singer who can follow more than one path' (Wemba 1994). Ironically Papa Wemba's CD, especially produced for his European audience won the prestigious Kora Award (the African equivalent to the Grammy)! As a general format, World Music standardizes certain musical traditions, while allowing at the same time for a unprecedented flowering and geographical spread of local musicians and styles. The differentiation of world music rapidly advances as the demand for non-Western music increases and competition among labels creates further openings for new producers and artists.

References

Barber, Karin and Christopher Waterman (1995). 'Traversing the Global and the Local: Fují Music and Praise Poetry in the Production of Contemporary Yoruba Popular Culture.' In: Miller, Daniel (ed.). *Worlds Apart*. London, 240–262.

Brown, Michael (1998). 'Can Culture be Copyrighted?' *Current Anthropology* 39 (2), 193–222.

Gillespie, Marie (1995). *Television, Ethnicity and Cultural Change*. London.

Lewis, Oscar (1951). *Life in a Mexican Village: Tepotzlán Restudied*. Champaign.

Marquez, Patricia C. (1999). *The Street is my Home. Youth and Violence in Caracas*. Stanford.

Martin, Emily (1994). *Flexible Bodies. Tracking Immunity in American Culture – From the Days of Polio to the Age of AIDS*. Boston.

Mead, Margaret (1962 [1950]). *Male and Female*. London.

Miller, Daniel (1989). *A Theory of Shopping*. Oxford.

Nader, Laura (1990). 'Orientalism, Occidentalism and the Control of Women.' *Cultural Dynamics*.

Papa Wemba (1994). 'Emotions.' *Realworld* (CD booklet).

Redfield, Robert (1930). *Tepoztlán: A Mexican Village*. Chicago.

Sahlins, Marshall (1988). 'Cosmologies of Capitalism: the Trans-Pacific Sector of the World System'. *Proceedings of the British Academy* LXXIV.

Seeger, Anthony (1997). 'Ethnomusicology and Music Law.' In: Ziff, Bruce and Rao, Pratima V. (ed.). *Borrowed Power. Essays on Cultural Appropriation*. New Brunswick, NJ: Rutgers University Press, 52–67.

Taylor, Timothy D. (1997). *Global Pop. World Music, World Markets*. London.

10 Globalization and communalization of music in the production perspective*

Richard A. Peterson

Numerous analysts of the processes of globalization and its opposite, here called communalization[1] have shown them to be inexorably linked. And what is more, their relationship seems to fit the dynamic of processes long central in the production of culture perspective.[2] It seems appropriate, therefore, to consider the dynamics of the production process in the context of globalization and dialectically linked communalization. To begin this analysis, we will define these two key concepts.

Introduction

The production perspective

The production perspective is based in the assertion that the social arrangements used in making symbolic elements of culture significantly shape the nature and content of the cultural elements that are produced. The production perspective is particularly relevant at the present time, because now, through their numerous divisions, just four global record firms control most of the music commercially distributed in the world, but now their hegemony is threatened by changes in the ways music is marketed and distributed to consumers.

The most widely researched dictum of the production perspective is that, irrespective of artistic creativity and fan preferences, when a cultural field like popular music is dominated by a few firms the music produced is more homogeneous, and when a large number of firms compete, the music is much more diverse.[3]

Since the idea was proposed by Peterson and Berger (1975), there have been a number of critiques based largely on changes in the way firms in the industry are organized. In particular, the massive multinational firms have learned to survive and prosper in the contemporary diverse market by taking the form of a number of distinct affiliated labels, each with a more or less distinct target audience delimited by age, gender, ethnicity, nationality, and political stance, as well as the aesthetic preferences of performers and fans. In the rapidly evolving market for popular music, the multinationals regularly take on, reconstitute, and discard labels to maintain a profitable position in all the niche markets that have been identified. Superficially at least, this distinction between large segmented firms and small producers seems to fit with the distinctions between globalism and communalism, but the parallel is not that neat.

Globalization

In recent years, a number of quite different meanings have been attached to the terms 'globalism' and 'globalization,' and in the process these are often used as little more than catch-words.[4] It is useful, therefore to state at the outset that my view of globalization is informed primarily by Zygmunt Bauman's provocative and profoundly pessimistic essay, 'Globalization: the Human Consequences,' published in 1997.

Globalization, for Bauman, is the current stage in the centuries-long process of the 'Western project,' focusing on industrialization, urbanization, bureaucratization, individuation and secularization. Globalization carries forward the ideas of the reciprocal relationship between *Gemeinschaft* and *Gesellschaft*. While early formulations saw the latter displacing the former, more recent formulations, such as that of World System theory, see that both survive while each is continually changed by its contact with the other. Contact with colonial nations, for example, helped to destabilize the colonized, but, at the same time, the presence of large numbers of slaves fundamentally marked the structures of slaver nations long after the end of chattel slavery.

At its core, globalization is an economic process in which capital, information, and elite persons are increasingly able to flow across physical boundaries in search of the most favorable short-term returns, and they can ever more easily retrace their steps as they please. The contemporary global elites are thus able to escape from situations where their actions have created impoverishment, civil unrest, and a despoiled environment. One of the prime reasons for Western colonialization in the second half of the second millennium has been the extraction of labor, fuel, food, and other raw materials from the colonized. In the current cosmopolitan atmosphere of 'one world, one culture,' the globalizers are also free to co-opt and incorporate elements of culture from outside the core of Western art and music. In the case of popular music, of course, most musical vitality is derived from the creative energies of disadvantaged groups.

Unlike the mobile elite, who are able to move freely because of their money, technical skills, and cultural capital, most people, because of insufficient economic, social and cultural capital, are physically stuck where they are, and their living standards move toward the average for the world population. This means that most of those in 'developed countries' experience lowering levels of real income and quality of life. At the same time, those in the 'developing world' do not experience a concomitant increase because there is less need for their manual skills and esoteric local knowledge. Through mass media programming and advertising, however, they do regularly see a picture of how the advantaged are supposed to live.

In an effort to resist the effects of globalization, marginalized populations turn to traditional identities and fabricate new communal allegiances of race, ethnicity, gender, religion, and language. But, as the theorists of globalization make clear, this does not mean simply returning to traditional *Gemeinschaft* roots. Rather traditions are invented and new local, tribal or communal styles are elaborated to fit the needs of the current political-cultural situation (Anderson 1983; Hobsbawm and Ranger 1983; Wallis and Malm 1984).

Some scholars celebrate the emancipatory potential of such 'resistance' (Hebdige 1979; Eyerman and Jamison 1998), and, in some cases the resistance has made for real change. A clear case in point is how the gay and lesbian community of New York dramatically outed itself through protest marches and flamboyant cultural displays in the late 1970s (DeChaine 1997). Nevertheless, such colorful gestures of resistance have more often been self-defeating (Willis 1977).

Tragically, most cultural resistance not only fails to achieve its original purpose, but it serves to awaken or reinforce antagonisms between groups, and these antagonisms most often serve the needs of political and economic interests hoping to profit from reconstituting religious, ethnic, gender, racial, territorial, and language distinctions for their own ends. Such anti-modernist groups have taken an array of forms including 'nationalism,' 'ethnic purity,' 'fundamentalism,' 'localism,' and 'neo-tribalism' but, in common, they emphasize the interests of a bounded community – however defined – over those of society as a whole. The term 'communal' seems best to fit them all.

As Bauman (1998) makes clear, the vitality of contemporary communal groups in the West and around the world is, ironically, a direct byproduct of globalization. The ideological fervor of such groups is regularly fed by appeals to the communal past but is reshaped and exacerbated by the economic and political dislocations coming in the wake of globalization. And curiously, while such communal groups regularly attack Americanization, the West, and capitalism, most of the energy they release is directed against neighboring communal groups. The increasingly virulent communal bloodletting in the nations of the West and around the world serve as ghastly cases in point.

Deconstructing globalization

Bauman grounds his formulation of globalization in the ideas that found their widest expression in the work of the *Frankfurt School* of the inter-war years of the twentieth century. One of their key concepts was that of massification. Observing the advance of the industrial revolution past the stage of craft production into the era of mass production by Henry Ford and others, they projected the logic of mass production onto all aspects of society and culture.

In this standardization, they saw authoritarian control and the de-individuation of the working classes into an undifferentiated and malleable mass. They identified the culture industry, and more particularly the mass media, as the prime agent of authoritarian control (Adorno and Horkheimer 1979). At the time, there seemed reason to fear the massifying power of the culture industry, because the radio was a prime tool of the powerful political demagogues of the time, Benito Mussolini, Adolph Hitler, Franklin Roosevelt, and Joseph Stalin.

Fifty years of subsequent evidence has shown that the mass media do not make for the massification of audiences. The evidence in our area of concern, popular music, provides an excellent case in point. While Adorno deplored the corrupting mindlessness of jazz, and Merton and Lazarsfeld warned of the narcotizing influence of radio-disseminated swing, a generation of research (some of it by those contributing to this anthology) has shown that audiences do not react as dumb masses, taking whatever fare is on offer, but select among offerings and reconstruct them to fit their own needs,[5] a process appropriately called the auto-production of culture (Peterson 1994a). It is for good reason therefore that we now use the term popular culture rather than mass culture.

Since from their elitist critical stance the Frankfurt School scholars profoundly misunderstood audiences as a dumb mass, they had no reason to study the inner workings of the culture industry either. If the audience was a mass that would accept any fare repeatedly fed to it, the mass culturalists reasoned, then clearly, following the logics of standardization and rationalization, the biggest firms could most nearly monopolize the sources of creation and distribution. On the other hand, if, as the popular culturalists suggested, people exercise considerable freedom of choice, then those firms will prosper that most consistently offer what people want. If the Frankfurt scholars had understood audience dynamics, they would have been led to see the battles that take place within the culture industry. This line of study, in practice, was only begun by the generation of 'production of culture' researchers who began publishing in the mid-1970s.

It is, of course, unfair to tar Zigmunt Bauman with the brush of the Frankfurt School; nonetheless, he, like they, does not go beyond an anecdotal engagement with the social, cultural, economic, and political processes driving globalization. Before leaving Bauman's view of globalization, however, it is important to recall that he sees the linked forces of globalization and communalization as equally destructive of the contemporary quality of human life. This is a vital observation because of our persistent tendency to romanticize the role of communal music producers and to demonize the large corporations (Frith 1996). The section that follows provides a scheme for understanding what the production perspective has to offer in better understanding how the globalizing and communalizing influences affect popular music.

Globalization of Music from the Production Perspective

The best ways to measure globalization are hotly debated.[6] Nevertheless, conjunction of globalizing and formalizing influences is suggested by data recently released by the International Federation of the Phonographic Industry. According to their reckoning, 64.6% of all recorded music was sold in the country where it was created, but the proportions vary widely from country to country. The countries that are the most 'local' are of two quite different sorts. On the one hand, they include the largest, highly competitive, and exporting markets, the United States with 91% and Japan with 78% locally produced music. On the other hand, among the countries for which data is available, Pakistan with 90%, Thailand with 82%, and Turkey 79%, are the most closed societies (IFPI 1999).[7]

Not for half a century has control of the world-wide music industry been as concentrated as in 2000. If anything, the industry is more concentrated now than in the late 1940s, when it reached its prior peak, because the market is much more nearly global in scope, and just four firms, BMG, Universal, Time-Warner, and Sony produce the bulk of all records sold in the world. Ironically, the picture looks quite different, however, if we move from *content* to *control of the content*. Here the dominance of the majors has not been so seriously threatened since the early days of the rock era (Ennis 1992; Peterson 1990).

The production perspective can be deployed to better understand the reasons for the rise of the global oligopoly and also the challenges it now faces. These can be understood by reviewing six major factors that, in interaction with each other, are central in shaping popular music. They include *law, technology, industry structure, organization structure, occupational careers*, and *market*. Because of my limited expertise, I will focus mostly on the US case beginning with the last mentioned factor, market.

Market

The market comprises the audience as seen from the perspective of the industry. Ironically, even the most experienced actors in the industry can never fully understand their audiences because their knowledge is based on samplings of information, and what they see is dependent on how the market has been conceptualized and how it is measured (Peterson 1994b; Anand and Peterson 2000). Both conceptualization and measurement are currently undergoing change.

For half a century the industry depended for market information on the weekly charts published by *Billboard* magazine and other industry sources that showed the performance of records relative to one another. The information was gathered by sales people in a sample of record sales outlets. Then in the early 1990s, *Billboard* began to rely on SoundScan point-of-sale information, collected automatically from cash registers (in the US), representing over 80% of all record sales. As Anand and Peterson (2000) show, it became much more difficult to fake sales figures, and this had both an immediate and a continuing impact on the nature of popular music. The new means of measuring record sales clearly showed that both rap and country music had much larger sales than had been reported before, and the influence of this new chart-defined view of the field continued in the years that followed, because suddenly these genres were seen to command big sales, much more money was put into marketing and promoting them, and their market shares expanded rapidly for several years.

If the advent of SoundScan affected the measurement of the market, another marketing tool may now be influencing how the markets are conceptualized. To rationalize marketing and distribution, it has been convenient to think of each market segment as being discrete (Ennis 1982). Thus, for example, the pop, country, alternative rock, dance, soul, jazz, etc. markets have been seen as separate entities – as if people who liked records classified in one music market category did not like music in any of the others, which we know is not true (Peterson and Kern 1995; 1996).

Again, using information from cash registers, (as well as purchasing patterns revealed in Internet sales) it is possible to construct recurrent patterns of individual choice. The music industry is far behind other consumer industries in using such information, but from informal work I have done with several students, it is clear that it is not very useful to think of country music fans, for example. Rather, it is more useful to think of country and gospel, country and heavy metal, country and middle-of-the road, or country and bluegrass fans, and the combinations are undoubtedly much more subtle (Peterson and Kern 1995).

Technology

Technological changes have always fostered developments in popular music. Take for example the question of who gets to be a successful pop music singer. At the beginning of the last century the barrel-chested operatic tenors such as Enrico Caruso were in ascendance because it took their classically trained big voices to be heard in the large concert halls and to successfully record the early acoustic phonograph records. Then with the use of microphones, both in large auditoriums and in cutting records, singers with small intimate 'natural' voices came to the fore. Led by Bing Crosby and Frank Sinatra, two generations of crooners were swept into prominence, and the lyrics of the new popular love song changed accordingly. Likewise, the emergence of Chicago-style blues, rockabilly, and rock cannot be understood without taking into account the development and elaboration of the electric guitar.

Currently the new technologies for the digital recording and transmission of music are profoundly reshaping popular music, allowing the computer to become the key musical instrument of the time. In the 1990s digital techniques of recording made it possible to sample, manipulate, and generate sound with a few keystrokes on the PC in myriad ways not possible in the era of analogue techniques. Collectively these have put more aesthetic control in the hands of engineers and producers at the expense of artists and performing groups (Ryan and Peterson 1994). Since the sounds performers generate can be altered and massaged, the vocal ability of singers is considerably less important, and this has put even more importance on the physical beauty and dance skills of the rising generation of performers. Likewise, technological developments in the manipulation of sound are central in the emergence of rap and essential to the wide panoply of evolving forms of dance music.

While it affects what music is made, the digitalization of sound also profoundly affects the broadcasting of music. Signals of radio stations are regularly sent on the Internet, so no matter where you are you can listen 'live' to the Grand Ole Opry from Nashville, the Metropolitan Opera from New York, or the Beijing Opera Company from China – just to name three among the wide range of choices. Seeing the potential of this medium, numerous 'stations' that do not broadcast at all now offer music on the Internet (Taylor 1999). Sitting in my garret office in Leeds, England, the world's music is now available at a touch. This example suggests globalization, but it can be a communalizing influence as well, when, for example, students resident in foreign countries around the world can surround themselves with the communal music of their motherland although they are tens of thousands of miles from home.

If the Internet provides the potential of infinitely variable 'virtual radio' programming, through MP3 and related technology, digitalization also offers a new means of distributing recorded music to fans. This technology is still in its infancy, but digitalization promises to make it possible to avoid the long established apparatus of retail record stores. Instead, one can download music directly to the computer hard drive or burn a CD copy to play later on conventional CD-playing equipment.

Industry structure, organization structure

In recent decades global corporations have consolidated their control of the music industry by using their control over the marketing and distribution of recorded music. In the process they have put out of business or absorbed most all of the intermediate and small companies that previously provided so much diversity in music. Through the last two decades of the twentieth century, the global companies responded to the consumer demand for a wide range of musics by continuing to issue CDs under a diverse range of labels (Lopes 1992; Scott 1999).

The digital system of music distribution described above makes it possible, in theory at least, for artists and fans to deftly avoid the apparatus of distribution through the global companies. If the majors lose their control, it will be impossible for the global music industry to exist in its present form. Predictably, the globals are moving to counter this possibility by ensuring that they control by using the strategies discussed below.

It seems most likely that the globals will be only partially successful in this effort, and it is interesting to contemplate the mix of organizational structures that may emerge to form the new industry structure, but this is all just now emerging and is, therefore, beyond the scope of this piece.

Ironically, another form of globalization can be seen at work here as well. No prior innovation before digital distribution has excited as much immediate attention among music research scholars around the world who are in touch with each other. In a few years, thanks to their efforts, the impacts of digital distribution on the structure of the music industry, on artists' careers, and on the music itself will be much more fully understood.

Occupational careers

At the present time there is a major difference between those artists who have contracts with the major companies and the vastly greater number who do not. Like the transnational corporations with whom they are affiliated, the former incur huge costs in the course of their work and may make large incomes, while the latter kind of communal artists incur low costs and may make a modest living from music (Wallis and Malm 1984; Robinson et al 1991; Guilbault 1993; Liew 1993; Lahusen 1993; Bennett 1999a: 73–194; Dawe 1999). If everyone can find an audience by offering their music via the Internet, the huge advantage held by artists signed to large labels disappears.

At the same time, if artists get exposure at the cost of giving away much of their music for free via the Internet, how will they make a living from their music? It is possible, for example, that all artists will use their recorded music as a means of promoting their live performances and receive the bulk of their income that way. This may seem implausible now, but this system of using media performance (via radio) to promote live performances was the prime means by which most musicians made a living before the Second World War (Peterson 1997).

Law and regulation

Consideration of law and regulation brings back into focus the nation-state, the entity that is generally defocalized in discussions of globalization. It is largely at the level of the nation-state that cultural policy formulated, broadcasting is regulated, censorship laws are shaped, and copyright regulations enforced (Cloonan 1999).

In a number of countries the content of music is directly censored by governments or those working in the name of the government. In Europe and North America such direct censorship is only sporadically practiced. Nonetheless, the threat of censorship is often made, and when well organized, quite effective in shaping musical expression and foreshortening musicians' careers. In the 1920s the bourgeois moral panic focused on jazz (Leonard 1962) and by the 1990s most was on rap and on dance music (Redhead 1993; 1995; Thornton 1995a; 1995b).

The impact of past technological innovations has been channeled and limited by the enactment and enforcement of a series of laws and regulations. Most of them have to do with the regulation of competition and the ownership of intellectual property (Peterson 1990). The struggles currently going on over distributing recorded music via the Internet are regularly couched as questions of intellectual property. More that any other set of influences, these will, I feel, shape popular music for the foreseeable future.

The major firms in the industry are aggressively trying to prevent the distribution of recorded music on the Internet, and at the same time, a legion of hackers are finding ways to elude their policing efforts. Industry firms are trying to perfect a technology called Secure Digital Music Initiative that is designed to make it impossible for anyone to make multiple copies from the music they control (Atwood 1999). Can it be circumvented? Will the multi-nationals and the digital distributors come to an accomodation? Or will another more decentralized logic of music production, distribution, and appreciation develop in the years to come? Answers to these questions are being hotly contested in the industry, among academic researchers, and in the popular media.[8]

Music field: Global industry/communal markets

Just as the general process of globalization has engendered new forms of localism, tribalism, or communalism, the increasingly global music firms have created a proliferation of uniquely structured niche music markets each appealing to a distinct consumer taste group. Such taste markets include the likes of rap, classical, boy-band teenie bop, jazz, blues, folk, musicals, dance techno, Bollywood, Latin, alternative rock, soul, gospel, country, Euro-pop, ethnic, and, since each has increasingly fragmented, many more niche markets as well. Each is distinct can be classed into types understood in terms of the ways its taste community is understood.

Music as structured taste groups

A number of scholars have found it useful to distinguish the distinctive ways in which taste group are structured and dynamically related. The three most often identified are: folk, popular, and fine art music (Peterson 1972; Frith 1996). While these distinctions are still useful, a four-fold classification may better represent early twenty-first century realities.

First, some music is *Mass-Marketed*. Such music is made only so long as it makes money. It is seen as a product targeted at a particular demographically defined market. Those in the music field readily equate 'the best' with the ones that have made them the most money. For their part, fans consume the music, using it to create a mood or an identity and dispose of it without a thought when it has served its purpose. Fans unreflectively say, 'I don't care what it is called, but I know what I like.' Examples of such mass-marketed music include: teen music, Muzak, Haydn for supermarkets, children's music, and the soft-shell end of all forms of music (Peterson 1997), whether opera, country, soul, new age, Euro-pop, jazz, or generic World music. In a sense, it is the music for those who don't like the real thing. Paradigmatic CDs targeted on the mass-market taste group include 'The Only Opera CD you Ever Need to Buy,' 'Classical Music for Lovers,' and 'Jazz for Idiots.'

Second, music may be made by and for people who share a common aesthetic based in *Group Identity*. Such an identity may be centered on one or more of the following: a place, a time, ethnicity, gender choice, language, life-style, and ideological commitment. Such music evokes a particular group identity, but may attract many artists and fans who at some level identify with, but are not members of the iconic group. Bluegrass, for example, celebrates the back-woods and conservative older rural ways of life, but, since the 1960s it has been embraced by many well-educated, liberal, urban players and fans (Rosenberg 1993; Eyerman and Jamison 1998). A number of music forms including blues, metal, dance, punk, hip-hop, and rockabilly are now sustained by fans who don't come from, but who identify with, the images and politics of the hard-core end of the genre (Peterson 1997).

Third, some genres have a *Creator-based Aesthetic*. Such music fields tend to place emphasis on the creative genius of composers and performers and have an institutionally grounded musical tradition appreciated by creators, critics, and aficionado fans as well. The forms, each of which has a well established and subsidized institutional system of support including musical organizations affiliated with performance halls, and schools where aspiring musicians and singers are trained and from which the aesthetic of the field is propagated to performers, professional critics and aficionado fans. In the twentieth century at least, these musics were seen to be vested with great moral value and of being worthy of private, government, and corporate subsidy. Symphonic, chamber, and choral music along with opera, are the most clear-cut cases, and jazz is well on its way to joining the set. Of all musics, those of this sort are the most nearly global in their aesthetic, so that, for example, performers trained in Peking, São Paulo, and Indianapolis can easily work together with other performers in Paris or Johannesburg.

The three types of music fields just outlined roughly follow the distinctions routinely made between popular, folk, and fine art music respectively. But now another way of structuring taste seems to be emerging. This has at its core a *Consumption-based Aesthetic*. Here music is included together by a music taste group as fitting a common ideologically-centered aesthetic commitment irrespective of the aesthetic within which the music was created. But I don't mean here readily accessible 'easy listening' or 'middle-of-the-road' music. John Schafer wrote a book in 1982 titled *New Sounds*. By 'new sounds' he did not mean newly composed pieces of music but the new soundscape that is created over the length of a musical experience such as a radio program. Thus, for example, on his own program he might juxtapose the music of a Bulgarian Women's chorus, Andean pan-pipes, Laurie Anderson's vocal distortions, and Trappist monks.

Alternative country music is a good example of the music of a consumption-based aesthetic. Alternative country is not so much a kind of music but an appreciation of a range of musics. Thus, an alternative country music program may juxtapose music made in the creators' aesthetic as bluegrass, rockabilly, grunge rock, singer-songwriter, and psychedelic California of the 1970s. What binds the musics is that all are seen as 'roots' music made by sincere artists who take a stance for self expression outside the commercial music mainstream (Goodman 1999; Peterson and Beal 2000). The eclectic folk music of Pete Seeger and those like him, as well as 'world music' as the term is used in some circles, also exemplify musics with a consumption-based aesthetic. Contemporary house, rave and techno dance musics also exemplify a kind of music built around a consumption-based aesthetic, in this case in a symbiosis between dance club DJs and dancers (Redhead 1998).

Having identified four ways of appreciating music and pointing to the quite different institutional systems elaborated around each, one must hasten to add that not all participants in a specific music field fit entirely into the same taste category. As Simon Frith et al. (1998) have observed, while a form of music may be identified with one, some people in each music field appreciate it in ways more typical of each of the other three forms of taste groups.

Some performers of even the crassest mass-marketed music, for example, become quite conscious of their music's social history and aesthetic parameters. At the same time, many who consume fine art music use it as a disposable entertainment or, alternatively, as a basis of cult fascination.[9]

Creating divisions facilitates globalization

In the 1940s and 1950s, each of the major record companies had a high degree of vertical integration with all the phases of music: making, from song writing and artist acquisition through to record distribution, carried out within the parent company under the banner of its name and logo. But in the years following the explosive success of rock 'n' roll the majors evolved the practice of developing a number of labels each devoted to a particular taste market (Lopes 1992; Burnett 1996; Peterson and Berger 1996; Cashmore 1997; Negus 1999).

This strategy allowed the majors to have a presence in flowering niche markets from rap to heavy metal, from chamber music to bhangra. The elaboration of more or less autonomous genre-based labels gave the major companies better contact with creative artists and also made it possible to divest its position in a genre of music as the demands of the market dictated. The multi-label policy also allowed the majors to produce more controversial records because they could exploit communal antipathies and still distance themselves whenever the cries for censorship became too great, as happened with gangsta rap in the 1990s (Jeffrey 1995; Negus 1999).

This division-creating strategy has also facilitated the globalization of the major firms because it has provided a model for ways of maintaining corporate hegemony while allowing flexibility to national and communal divisions.[10] Nonetheless, the global forms have not incorporated all kinds of music to the same degree, and the differences generally follow the lines dividing the four ways music tastes are organized that has just been discussed.

Mass-marketed musics are generally managed in-house, and the different labels under which records are issued are simply brand names created to target, promote, and successfully market the music. Music based in group identity, on the other hand, generally is produced and marketed by more or less autonomous labels within a country and around the world (Burnett 2001; Malm 2001). Thus, for example, the labels releasing rap music in France, Germany, and in Sweden are not the same as those in the United States (Bennett 1999). Music genres produced according to a creator-based aesthetic, such as classical music and opera, are generally produced by semi-autonomous divisions as well, but these, following the music genres themselves, tend to have a world-wide scope. Finally, the global corporations do not generally understand the logic of consumption-based communal music as a market and so do not enter these fields.[11]

Globalism and communalism of music

Music commentators, even some who work for the music industry press, decry the impact that the global corporations have on popular music. To be sure, they often act like rapacious but clumsy dinosaurs who gobble up or crush the smaller mammals in their midst, but they create the environment that has allowed generations of independent firms to grow and evolve. The potential of Internet-based distribution make possible an environment in which the global firms may become extinct in the foreseeable future, but socialist sponsorship and control, the other major way of organizing popular music fields in the twentieth century, hardly proved more propitious for the autonomous development of music.[12]

Simon Frith (1996) has reminded us that rock, like all forms of pop music, was part of a business and commercial from the outset. Nonetheless, we music researchers tend to side with the small firms that championed the sorts of music that first whetted our love of music and to put down all change to corrupting influences of the global firms without. This view does not take into consideration the fact that all musical styles flower and fade just as all generations have their day and pass.[13]

To be sure many independent companies are bought and absorbed, but others become ideologically attuned to the community that supports them and continue to prosper outside the global industry. Many more die of natural causes because they are not in tune with any community, because they grow old, lose touch and fade with their communal generation, or self-destruct in a flurry of bad managerial decisions. In any case, virtually no independents maintain their viability beyond the active life of their founding members.

* * *

Having outlined the workings of the contemporary music industry through the production perspective, we can now return briefly to the subject with which we began: popular music in the context of globalization. It is vital in this age of globalization, not to romanticize communally-oriented musics with which we can identify even though they may take an ideologically or aesthetically resistant stance toward mass-marketed music. Zygmunt Bauman has shown that the general process of globalization brings in its wake a welter of revitalized and virulent forms of jingoistic communal interests – each contending more with the others around it than with the globalizers.

Two examples must suffice. In the late 1970s, the discontents of American punk rockers were fanned into virulent hatred rallying behind the slogan, 'disco sucks.' On the surface this was a dispute over musical aesthetics, but just below the surface the movement was a disempowered young white male ranting against a form of music that empowered women, blacks, and gays with middle-class consumerist expectations (Peterson 1978; Redhead 1998).

Second, as reported by Barber-Kersovan in this anthology, the music industry in the successor states of Yugoslavia provides chilling evidence that local
independent firms can both profit from and propagate communal animosities
through the creation of newly composed 'folk songs,' their corresponding
dance forms such as 'Turbo Folk,' and vivid jingoistic pop music videos.

Zygmunt Bauman's ironic formulation of the communalizing consequences of globalization suggest a more complex dialectic between global
industry and communal forms of music than is proposed in most formulations. Here we have explored some of the ways in which a focus on the production of culture can help to better understand the dynamics of the global-
communal interplay.

Notes

*   My understanding of globalization has benefited greatly from conversations with Zigmunt Bauman and with the University of Leeds' Social Theory Group, while my
thoughts on music today have been sharpened by Andy Bennett, Robert Burnett, Alenka
Barber-Kersovan, Krister Malm, Keith Negus, Claire Peterson, Keith Roe, John Ryan
and members of my 1999–2000 University of Leeds 'Music in Society' course. The statements made here should, however, in no way be taken as representing their views.

1   A number of terms have been used to represent the opposite of 'globalization.' Here we
will us 'communal' because it seems to be the least evaluative. The term 'local' or 'tribal'
will be used as a special case of the communal when appropriate (Maffesoli 1996).

2   This relationship is illustrated, for example, by the chapters in this anthology by Burnett,
Negus, Roe, and Malm.

3   On the relationship between the structure of the music industry and the kinds of music
produced, see: Peterson and Berger 1975, Peterson 1990, Burnett 1990, Lopes 1992, and
Negus 1997; 1999.

4   On uses of the meaning of globalization see in particular: Appadurai 1996, Bauman
1997, Bennett 1999b, Braman et al. 1996, Featherstone 1990, Tomlinson 1999, and especially Held et al. 1999.

5   For studies showing the ways people make mass produced Their own see for example:
Denisoff and Peterson 1972, Hall and Jefferson 1976, Hebdige 1979, Frith 1981, Chambers 1985, Redhead 1990, Goodwin 1992, Lahusen 1993, Liew 1993, Epstein 1994, Peterson 1994a, Rose 1994, Ellison 1995, Thornton 1995a, DeChaine 1997, Bennett 1999a
and Dawe 1999.

6   See for example the articles by Gebesmair in this anthology.

7   No data was available from many of the most closed countries including Burma, Iran,
and Afghanistan. The United Kingdom, which is near the median of all the countries surveyed, offers an interesting case of the cross-press between globalization and communalization. Second only to the US, it is the greatest exporter of music, but at the same time,
much of the music sold in the UK is imported from the US (IFPI 1999).

8   For a sampling of industry comment see Atwood 1999, Gillen & Jeffrey 1999, Hillis
1999; for academic discussion see Lange 1999, Witte and Howard 1999, Hutter 2000,
Marshall 2000; and for several views published in the popular press see Goodman 1999,
Gomes 1999, Hellmore 2000.

9   This is not the place to give detailed examples, but one cross-over, that of fine art music
used as communal music may seem unlikely. But communities of fans may coalesce
around an interest in one creator or school of music. When I was an undergraduate

student at Oberlin College, for example, there were a number of such groups. Examples include the Mahler-Bruckner Circle and the group of young men who coalesced around the harpsichord playing of Wanda Lindowska.

10   In practice the degree of autonomy is much lower than it might be because of bureaucratic pressures for sticking to one way of working across all corporate divisions (Negus 1999, 2001; Burnett 1996, 2001).

11   This is not to say that individual artists considered alternative country, for example, do not have contracts with the major corporations, but, to date, no labels or divisions have been created around the aesthetic of alternative country music.

12   Few outside authoritarian religious and political establishments would argue the merits of Soviet or puritanical systems for producing music, but, in a different legal and administrative environment, innovation might have been fostered without stifling control (Becker 1982, Wallis and Malm 1984, Guilbault 1993, Manuel 1993, Held et al 1999).

13   The pitfalls of treating popular culture as if it was just a form of art culture are explored by Frith and Savage (1998) and are seen by Peterson and Kern (1996) as central to an emerging way of reconfiguring the relationship between aesthetic taste and social status.

References

Adorno, Theodor W. and Max Horkheimer (1979). *Dialectic and Enlightenment*. London: Verso.

Anand, N. and Richard A. Peterson (2000). 'When Market Information Constitutes Fields: Sensemaking of Markets in the Commercial Music Field.' *Organization Science*.

Anderson, B. (1983). *Imagined Communities*. London: Verso.

Appadurai, A. (1996). *Modernity at Large: Cultural Dimensions of Globalization*. Minneapolis: University of Minnesota Press.

Atwood, Brett (1999). 'Labels, Artists Clash over MP3.' *Billboard* May 1:1, 74.

Banks, J. (1996). *Monopoly Television: MTV's Quest to Control the Music*. Boulder, CO: Westview.

Bauman, Zygmunt (1998). *Globalization: The Human Consequences*. Oxford: Polity.

Becker, Howard S. (1982). *Art Worlds*. Berkeley: University of California Press.

Bennett, Andy (1999a). *Popular Music and Youth Culture: Music, Identity and Practice*. London: Macmillan.

Bennett, Andy (1999b). 'Subcultures or Neo-tribes? Rethinking the Relationship between Youth, Style and Musical Taste.' *Sociology* 33, 599–617.

Braman, S. and A Sreberny-Mohammandi, editors (1996). *Globalization, Communication and Transnational Civil Society*. Cresskill, NJ: Hampton Press.

Burnett, Robert (1990). *Concentration and Diversity in the International Phonogram Industry*. Gothenburg, Sweden: University of Gothenburg Press.

Burnett, Robert (1996). *The Global Jukebox*. London: Routledge.

Burnett, Robert (2001). 'Global strategies and local markets.' In this anthology.

Cashmore, Ellis (1997). *The Black Culture Industry*. London: Routledge.

Chambers, Iain (1985). *Urban Rhythms: Pop Music and Popular Culture*. London: Macmillan.

Cloonan, Martin (1997). 'State of the Nation: "Englishness": Pop and Politics in the Mid-1990s.' *Popular Music and Society* 21: 2, 47–70.

Cloonan, Martin (1999). 'Pop and the Nation-State: Toward a Theorization.' *Popular Music* 18, 193–207.

Dawe, Kevin (1999). 'Minotaurs or Musonauts? "World Music" and Cretan Music.' *Popular Music* 18, 209–225.

DeChaine, D. Robert (1997). 'Mapping Subversion: Queercore Music's Playful Discourse of Resistance.' *Popular Music and Society* 21:1, 7–38.

Denisoff, R. Serge and Richard A. Peterson (1972). *The Sounds of Social Change*. Chicago: Rand McNally.
Devereaux, Scott (1997). *The Birth of Bebop: A Social and Musical History*. Berkeley: University of California Press.
Ellison, Curtis W. (1995). *Country Music Culture*. Jackson: University Press of Mississippi.
Ennis, Philip (1992). *The Seventh Stream*. Hanover, NH: University Press of New England.
Epstein, Jonathon S. (ed.) (1994). *Adolescents and their Music: If It's Too Loud, You're Too Old*. New York: Garland.
Eyerman, Ron and Andrew Jamison (1998). *Music and Social Movements*. Cambridge: University of Cambridge Press.
Featherstone, Mike (1990). *Global Culture*. London: Sage.
Frith, Simon (1981). *Sound Effects: Youth Leisure and the Politics of Rock 'N' Roll*. New York: Pantheon.
Frith, Simon (ed.) (1993). *Music and Copyright*. Edinburgh: University of Edinburgh Press.
Frith, Simon (1996). *Performing Rites*. Cambridge: Harvard University Press.
Frith, Simon and Jon Savage (1998). 'Pearls and Swine: Intellectuals and the Mass Media.' In: Steve Redhead (ed.). *The Subcultures Reader*. London: Blackwell, 7–17.
Garofalo, Rebe (1997). *Rockin' Out: Popular Music in the USA*. Boston: Allyn & Bacon.
Gillen, Marilyn and Don Jeffrey (1999). 'Web Biz Models Debated.' *Billboard* July 31, 1,96.
Gilmore, Samuel (1988). 'Schools of Activity and Innovation.' *Sociological Quarterly* 29, 203–219.
Goodman, Fred (1999). 'Is MP3 the End of the Music Business?' *Rolling Stone* April 1, 25–28.
Goodwin, Andrew (1992). *Dancing in the Distraction Factory: Music Television and Popular Culture*. Minneapolis: University of Minnesota Press.
Gomes, Lee (1999). 'MP3 Music Moves Into the High-School Mainstream.' *Wall Street Journal* June 15, B1,B4.
Guilbault, Jocelyne (1993). *Zouk: World Music in the West Indies*. Chicago: University of Chicago Press.
Hall, S. and Tony Jefferson (1976). *Resistance Through Rituals: Youth Subcultures in Post-War Britain*. London: Hutchinson.
Hebdige, Dick. (1979). *Subculture: The Meaning of Style*. London: Methuen.
Held, D., A. McGrew, D. Goldblatt, and J. Perraton (1999). *Global Transformations*. Cambridge: Polity.
Hellmore, Edward (2000). 'Music Industry Is Caught Napping.' *Guardian* March 16 Online: 10.
Hillis, Scott (1999). 'Public Enemy Uses Internet to Fight Music Industry.' *Variety* May 29.
Hirst, P. and G. Thompson (1996). *Globalization in Question*. Cambridge: Polity.
Hobsbawm, Eric and Terence Ranger (1983). *The Invention of Tradition*. Cambridge: Cambridge University Press.
Hutter, Michael (2000). 'The Effect of the Internet on the Culture Industries.' Unpublished manuscript. Baden-Baden, Germany.
IFPI (1999). *The recording industry in numbers 99*. London: ifpi.
Jeffrey, D. (1995). 'Warner's Fuchs Pledges Scrutiny.' *Billboard* October 14:1, 19.
Lahusen, Christian (1993). 'The Aesthetics of Radicalism: The Relationship Between Punk and the Patriotic Nationalist Movement of the Basque Country.' *Popular Music* 12: 263–280.
Laing, Dave (1985). *One Chord Wonders: Power and Meaning in Punk Rock*. Milton Keynes, UK: Open University Press.
Lange, David (1999). 'At Play in the Field of the Word: Copyright and the Construction of Authorship in the Post-Literate Millennium.' *Law and Contemporary Problems* 55, 2.
Leonard, Neil (1962). *Jazz and the White Americans*. Chicago: University of Chicago Press.

Liew, Maria van (1993). 'The Scent of Catalan Rock: Els Pets' Ideology and the Rock and Roll Industry.' *Popular Music* 12, 245–261.

Lopes, Paul (1992). 'Innovation and Diversity in the Popular Music Industry,' *American Sociological Review* 57, 56–71.

Maffesoli, Manuel (1996). *The Time of the Tribes: The Decline of Individualism in Mass Society.* London: Sage.

Malm, Krister (2001). 'Globalization – localization, homogenization – diversification and other discordant trends: A challenge to music policy makers.' In this anthology.

Manuel, Peter L. (1993). *Cassette Culture: Popular Music and Technology in North India.* Chicago: University of Chicago Press.

Marshall, Lee (2000). 'The Future of the Bootleg Aesthetic.' Unpublished manuscript. Sociology: University of Warwick.

Negus, Keith (1997). 'The Production of Culture.' In: P. Du Guy (ed.). *Production of Culture/ Cultures of Production.* Milton Keynes, UK: Open University Press.

Negus, Keith (1999). *Music Genres and Corporate Cultures.* London: Routledge.

Negus, Keith (2001). 'Structures and strategies of the transnational music and media industry.' In this anthology.

Peterson, Richard A. (1972). 'A Process Model of the Folk, Pop, and Fine Art Stages of Jazz.' In: *American Music: From Storyville to Woodstock*, edited by Charles Nanry. New Brunswick, NJ: Rutgers University Press, 135–151.

Peterson, Richard A. (ed.) (1976). *The Production of Culture.* Beverly Hills, CA: Sage.

Peterson, Richard A. (1978). 'Disco! Its Distinctive Sound Isn't Just Another Fad.' *Chronicle of Higher Education* October 2, 26–27.

Peterson, Richard A. (1990). 'Why 1955? Explaining the Advent of Popular Music.' *Popular Music* 9, 97–116.

Peterson, Richard A. (1994a). 'Cultural Studies through the Production Perspective: Progress and Prospects.' In: Diana Crane (ed.). *The Sociology of Culture.* Oxford: Blackwell, 163–190.

Peterson, Richard A. (1994b). 'Measured Markets and Unknown Audiences: Case Studies from the Production and Consumption of Music.' In: James S. Ettema and D. Charles Whitney (eds.). *Audiencemaking: How the Media Create the Audience.* Newbury Park, CA: Sage, 171–185.

Peterson, Richard A. (1997). *Creating Country Music: Fabricating Authenticity.* Chicago: University of Chicago Press.

Peterson, Richard A. and Bruce A. Beal (2000). 'Alternative Country: Origins, Music, World-View, Fans, and Taste in Genre Formation.' *Popular Music In Society.* Forthcoming.

Peterson, Richard A. and David G. Berger (1975). 'Cycles in Symbol Production: The Case of Popular Music.' *American Sociological Review* 40, 158–173.

Peterson, Richard A. and David G. Berger (1996). 'Measuring Industry Concentration, Diversity, and Innovation in Popular Music.' *American Sociological Review* 61, 175–178.

Peterson, Richard A. and Roger Kern (1995). 'Hard-Core and Soft-Shell Country Fans.' *The Journal of Country Music* 17: 3, 3–6.

Peterson, Richard A. and Roger Kern (1996). 'Changing High-Brow Taste: From Snob to Omnivore' *American Sociological Review* 61, 900–907.

Redhead, Steve (1990). *The End-of-the-Century Party: Youth and Pop Toward 2000.* Manchester: Manchester University Press.

Redhead, Steve (1993). *Rave-off: Politics and Deviance in Contemporary Youth Culture.* Aldershot, UK: Avebury.

Redhead, Steve (1995). *Unpopular Cultures: The Birth of law and Popular Culture.* Manchester: Manchester University Press.

Redhead, Steve, ed. (1998). *The Clubcultures Reader.* London: Blackwell.

Robinson, Deanna Campbell, Elizabeth B. Buck, and Marlene Cuthbert (1991). *Music at the Margins.* Newbury Park, CA: Sage.

Roe, Keith (1993). 'Academic Capital and Music Tastes Among Swedish Adolescents: An Empirical Test of Bourdieu's Model of Cultural Reproduction.' *Young: The Nordic Journal of Youth Research.* 1: 3, 44–55.

Rose, Tricia (1994). *Black Noise: Rap Music and Black Culture in Contemporary America.* Hanover, NH: University Press of New England.

Rosenberg, Neil V. (ed.) (1993). *Transforming Tradition: Folk Music Revival Examined.* Urbana: University of Illinois Press.

Ryan, John and Richard A. Peterson (1994). 'Occupational and organizational consequences of the digital revolution in music making.' In: Muriel Cantor and Sheryl Zollars (eds). *Cretors of Culture.* Greenwich, CT: JAI Press, 173–201.

Scott, A. J. (1999). 'The US Recorded Music Industry: On the Relations Between Organization, Location, and Creativity in the Cultural Economy.' *Environment and Planning* 31, 1965–1984.

Shevory, Thomas C. (1995). 'Bleached Resistance: The Politics of Grunge.' *Popular Music and Society* 19: 2, 23–48.

Taylor, Chuck (1999). 'Webcasters Reshape Radio Landscape.' *Billboard* June 5: 1, 133.

Thornton, Sarah (1995a). *Club Cultures: Music, Media and Subcultural Capital.* Cambridge: Polity.

Tomlinson, J. (1999). *Globalization and Culture.* Cambridge: Polity Press.

Wallis, Roger and Krister Malm (1984). *Big Sounds from Small Peoples: The Music Industry in Small Countries.* London: Constable.

Weinstein, Denna (1991). *Heavy Metal: A Cultural Sociology.* New York: Macmillan.

Willis, Paul (1977). *Learning to Labour.* Farnborough, UK: Saxon House.

Witte, James and Philip Howard (1999). 'Digital Citizens and Digital Consumers: Demographic Transition on the Internet.' Unpublished manuscript. Evanston, IL: Northwestern University.

11 Measurements of globalization: Some remarks on sources and indicators

Andreas Gebesmair

Keeping in mind that globalization of music is a complex process which is constrained by a variety of different factors, I'd like to pose the question which arises in this context in a very simple way: how is music affected by changes in the structure of the transnational music industry? Without trying to give any answer to this widely discussed question within this paper it should be the starting point of some considerations about the measurement of globalization, especially the availability, reliability and validity of data which could serve as appropriate indicators.

Studies on the music industry which aim to provide a comprehensive empirical description are limited by the availability of statistical materials. Though the situation has improved since the beginnings of research on culture industries students continue to complain about the lack of reliable data. The collection and processing of data always lags behind the demand for an empirical scrutiny of contemporary theories. The Finnish sociologist Pekka Gronow wrote in his study on the record industry prepared for the Mediacult institute in the first half of the 70s:

> Quite unfortunately, there have been very few serious investigations of the phonographic record industry since Schulz-Köhn's work, which appeared in 1940. The best sources of information are still trade publications and data from the industry itself, such as from the International Federation of the Phonographic Industry. Even this material is often difficult to obtain and is not published in compiled form. Very little is known about the sales shares of domestic and imported phonograph albums in different countries, to say nothing of the sales figures for individual genres. The data which are available on the use of recorded music on the radio and on jukeboxes is even more meager (Gronow, quoted in Blaukopf 1977: 21 [re-translated from the German]).

Fifteen years later Keith Negus stated in his pioneering study on the popular music industry:

> Although the major record companies place considerable importance on their market share, they are very secretive about revealing information. An accountant

I spoke to at one of the transnationals told me that, although they were available "somewhere", reliable figures could probably only be obtained after "high level corporate detective work" (Negus 1992: 156).

Nevertheless, theoretical considerations on the development of music in the era of globalization should rest on reliable empirical data. In the following I will present some sources which could be used for studying the globalization of music. I'd like to deal with some methodological questions concerning these sources in four steps:

First, some general remarks will touch on the question of how terms like 'music industry' or 'music' could be translated into a measurable form.

Second, I will identify some appropriate indicators which are commonly used in relevant literature and studies on the music industry.

Third, I'd like to refine the starting question and provide two models regarding the impact of globalization on music.

Fourth, I'd like to evaluate some selected indicators with regard to their availability, validity and reliability.

What does 'music industry' and 'music' mean?

As mentioned above we can put the question about the impact of globalization on music in a more general way: How is music affected by changes in the structure of the transnational music industry? In order to get a clear picture of the globalization process we have to regard both sides of that simple causal relationship between music and music industry separately. The transnational orientation and organization of the music industry has to be distinguished analytically from the globalization of music which refers to the global distribution of music as a commodity as well as to its 'hybridization'.

The music industry

Several definitions are suggested according to different concepts of the music industry. Some students described the music industry in terms of systems in which major companies flexibly incorporate or establish links to semi-autonomous (independent) labels or subsidiaries and try to adapt to a changing environment: to new media and distribution technologies, new market structures, changing taste structures, laws, etc. (Hirsch 1972, Peterson and Berger 1975, Peterson 1990, Lopez 1992, Christianen 1995, Burnett 1996). It is impossible to elaborate comprehensively on these conceptions in our context. For now, I'd like to point out some indicators used in these studies on the music industry:

The most debated feature of the music industry is its *concentration*, which refers to the actual market share of the main companies in a given market.

Most studies on this subject use the four-, six- or eight-firm index which simply adds the market shares of the four, six or eight largest corporations. For instance Peterson and Berger (1975), Lopes (1992) and Burnett (1996) calculated these indicators by adding the number of hits produced by one company within a year using billboard charts, others (e.g. Christianen 1995) prefer figures about market shares as provided from IFPI (International Federation of the Phonographic Industry) arguing that these figures represent the whole market and not only a small segment as represented in the charts.

These measures could be calculated for regional and national markets as well as for the world market. The more markets that show the same characteristics, that means that a few corporations (major labels) dominate different markets all over the world, the more globalized is the market. This should be highlighted: Concentration in single markets doesn't necessarily indicate internationalization or globalization of the music industry. The five biggest record companies of the world (BMG, EMI, Warner, Sony, Universal) are supposed to account for more than 80% of the world market. This somehow mystical figure which would be difficult to check seems evident for the European and US markets. But there are still huge markets like China and India which resist the expansion of Western music industries. Even in a strong market like Japan the above mentioned major labels only accounted for about 50% in 1997 (MBI 1999).

Furthermore, the impact of the music industry's concentration on the musical repertoire seems to not be very strong. Though this assumption has to be proved a first look at the sound carriers sold in different markets with a different amount of concentration shows that the diversity of music is not directly affected by the industry's concentration. Since the major labels increasingly satisfy local demands high concentration could be accompanied by a great deal of local music production. For instance in Brazil where the music market is dominated by the big four domestic repertoire accounts for about 50% of total national music retail sales.

Therefore, a further feature of the music industry should be taken into account: its *internal competition* (Burnett 1996). Due to the fact that single departments and subsidiaries are competing more and more within a corporation at a high level of market concentration, it is necessary to measure the amount of this internal competition. Christianen (1995) proposes to count the number of decision-makers within a firm.

This could show the way to measure features like transnationalization or *globalization* of music companies *on the organizational level*. The number of subsidiaries in different countries and the number of autonomous decision makers in these subsidiaries reflects quite well the global orientation of a company. Decisions about repertoire are not only made in the headquarters of the companies which are pushing a certain repertoire but on different levels all over the world.

The degree of 'autonomy' or 'independence' is the crucial point in the study of globalization. An indicator of internationalization (e.g. the number of subsidiaries in different countries) could be interpreted in two completely different ways. While high numbers of strongly *dependent* subsidiaries which carry out orders from headquarters and function mainly as local distributors of international repertoire suggest a music industry according to the cultural imperialism thesis (Laing 1986), a high number of *independent* subsidiaries or of joint ventures with independent labels which are in a position to develop their own local repertoire supports the assumption of global exchange systems and hence the picture of a really 'transnational music industry'.

Whilst surveys on numbers of subsidiaries or sublabels could be performed rather easily (most major companies provide information about their global organization on their web sites), it is hard to measure the kind of organizational independence. The credibility for instance of single A&Rs (artist & repertoire manager) and his/her chance to push the artists under contract depends on factors which are not easy to explain. Walter Gröbchen (A&R manager with BMG-Hamburg): 'The chance to get an adequate marketing budget to promote your products depends on your weight within the company, your personal history of success and your self-assertion.' Regarding the relationship to other regional departments of the same major label (especially in the UK and the USA): 'normally they don't listen to any of our stuff' (i.e. Austrian or German acts) (Mediacult 1998).

Maybe the depiction of the music industry as an open system overestimates the degree of 'independence' of local subsidiaries. Anyway, the analysis of the organizational structure of the transnational music industry and the construction of appropriate indicators on this subject is an important task and a prerequisite for answering the question how music is effected by the globalization of culture industries.[1]

Music

Let's move on to the second term in our starting question, the music. I propose to distinguish between music as a symbolic form and music as a commodity.

Dealing with music as a *symbolic form* is the way musicologists commonly consider music. Several methods have been developed to describe music especially historical ('classical') music. At the University of Vienna we learned a method of style analysis that has been used by musicologists since the end of the last century and which handles only written music concerning its structure. When analyzing pop music, we have to take into account that most of its music is not written but rather a recorded performance. One of the main dimensions is its sound, which is not represented in conventional systems of music writing. By the end of the 1950s the French musicologist

Abraham A. Moles (1971) introduced a method with which features like complexity of technical reproduced music could be quantified by relying on an information theory. Later on this technique was applied to pop and rock music (Niketta 1985, Dowd 1992).

In the study of globalization, a great challenge to music analysis is how to relate a musical text to a certain territory or ethnicity. The simplest way to define the regional or ethnical identity of a musical piece is to look at the language it is performed in. But as students of regional popular music have noticed, what is sung in Russian or Italian often is a kind of *de-anglicization* (Larkey 1993) or *imitation* (Regev 1997) of a global accepted US-American rock aesthetic.

Nevertheless, since the 1970s a wide range of so called *hybrids* have emerged all over the world (e.g. Wallis and Malm 1984, Mitchell 1993, Regev 1997). Rock elements are selectively adapted and mixed with traditional, local styles. Regev assumes that 'practitioners of such hybrid musics sometimes do not even have to claim their "local authenticity". It is inscribed in the essence of the sonic texture and affective impact' (Regev 1997: 134). But what remains to be explained is what musical forms, what kind of rhythm, which voices, sounds and instruments are recognized as Afro-American, Algerian or Indian.[2]

This leads to another point which should be mentioned: Musical artifacts are interpreted or – as representatives of Cultural Studies call it – decoded differently in different contexts. As students of culture have illustrated, the 'meaning' of music occurs in a complex process of usage in everyday life. While one decodes a certain music style as representing the identity of a certain region, others may listen to it regardless of its supposed identity. For instance Latin Music genres signify certain diaspora cultures in the USA, whereas for white listeners in Europe it may be only another kind of pop music with some exotic colour.

These remarks should serve as a short reference to problems we face when analyzing the territorial or ethnical significance of music on the symbolic level. Therefore it seems to be easier (at first glance) to look at music as a *commodity*.

Music is a commodity which is produced, manufactured, distributed, broadcasted, sold and purchased and some times illegally distributed, copied or simply stolen. Thus we can regard music as a commodity. Like all commodities, music too can be measured in terms of units and values. This provides a number of useful and suitable indicators which indicate the global flow of music.

Indicators[3]

The graph entitled 'Commodity flow and indicators' provides a framework for locating different parameters of measurement (cf. Figure 11.1). This sketch comprises different conceptions of the music industry, especially

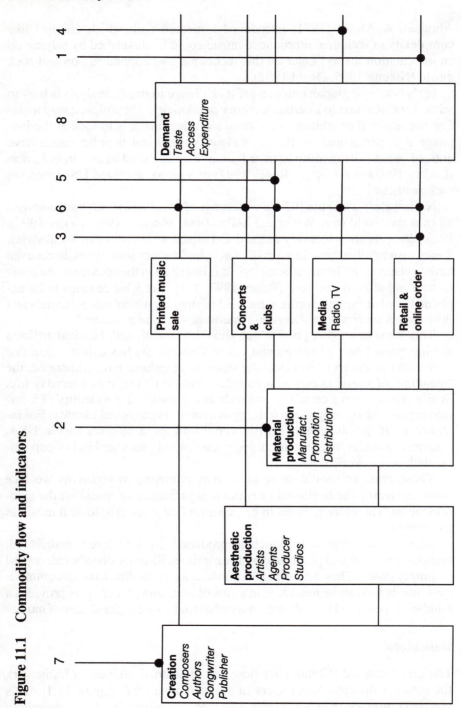

Figure 11.1   Commodity flow and indicators

Hirsch's System of Pre-Selection (Hirsch 1969; see also graphs in Fink 1996 and Hull 1998). The single sections represent different filters in the process of pre-selection which music has to run through before final consumption. Of course there are manifold interrelations between the parts of this system and the music is not only admitted or excluded at every stage but undergoes changes within this process, as Negus has mentioned (Negus 1992). Nevertheless, keeping in mind that this depiction is incomplete (especially the emerging Internet distribution is not regarded) and imprecise (the filters intersect on every stage of the process) it serves as a useful framework for distinguishing certain indicators.

When analyzing globalization this distinction is crucial since the single stages and levels indicate different parts of society and different forms of distribution of music. If we look for instance at retail charts provided by the trade magazine Billboard we might recognize the homogenization of global repertoires. The pool of international acts which are pre-selected by a complex system of producers, agents, marketing managers, media gatekeepers, retailers and last but not least the consumer demand is becoming smaller and smaller and dominates charts in more and more countries all over the world (although the trend is not as obvious as suggested here.) At the same time we can assume that beyond these media and retail filters a wide range of sound carriers are manufactured yearly which might find their way to the listeners – or solely fill up the stock rooms without being sold. The same might be true on the level of aesthetic production regardless of whether the artists produce sound carriers or not. According to Christianen (1995) we can describe this pre-selection system as a pyramid with a high diversity of artists and aesthetic production at the bottom and a small number of single hits at the top. When using different indicators we probably face contradictory effects of the globalization process: While the supply with sound carriers of diverse origin is increasing on a local level, the small number of vastly demanded mega-acts more and more dominate the international repertoire of the major industry.

Available indicators are shortly described in the following list:

1. *Sale of sound carriers* This is the most frequent source used in popular music research and usually provided by IFPI (International Federation of the Phonographic Industry) or national organizations of the phonographic industries. Since so many students rely on these data, IFPI's statistics deserve special scrutiny.

Retail charts Charts play a very important role in popular music research, especially in the 'production of culture' approach. Besides retail charts, there are also airplay charts (cf. No. 4) and combinations of both. Since charts are computed in different ways they too need some remarks on reliability.

Awards (Gold, Platinum) While retail charts represent bestsellers within a certain time span (e.g. one week) Gold or Platinum are awarded for an accumulated amount of sold sound carriers, which differs from country to country. Sales of one million sound carriers are required for Platinum in the USA, only 50,000 in Austria.

Piracy Beside the legitimate pre-selection system there is also an illegal retail of sound carriers whose impact on the globalization of music has to be evaluated. Unfortunately most available figures are estimates which serve as horror scenario to support the record industry's anti-piracy policy. Therefore they aren't very reliable.

2. *New releases and available sound carriers ('catalogues')* As mentioned above, looking at different stages of the filter process we may observe different phenomena of globalization and homogenization. In his 1995 study Christianen deploys figures about the amount of new releases in the Dutch music industry. Studying the effect of the music industry's structure on diversity, he argues that we should consider all available records and not only the top 10 albums and singles which run through several filters as media, retail and consumer demand. He used data compiled at the Stichting Centrale Discothek in the Netherlands which also includes information about genre and national origin. Similar databases exist in many countries since meanwhile orders of records are placed electronically using catalogues on the Internet (for instance *phononet* in Germany and Austria). Additionally, we have to consider independent distributors with their special catalogues, some of them available electronically.

Manufactured sound carriers Pekka Gronow points to the industrial statistics of the United Nations Organisation, which also includes figures for 'gramophone records' (Gronow). Similar statistics are available from local or regional statistical offices (e.g. EUROSTAT). Since there isn't any additional information about the repertoire and because the surveys are based on samples these kind of statistics do not provide useful information on the production and global distribution of popular music.

3. *Delivered sound carriers* Sometimes figures about the delivery to retailers, called wholesale values, are published regardless of whether the sound carriers are purchased by consumers. These figures indicate the flow of commodity in front of the demand filter!

4. *Airplay charts* Airplay charts are generally measured before the filter of demand, for which computerized 'fingerprints' have been employed recently. But these measurements also consider the range of different radio stations; therefore consumer demand has an impact on airplay charts. They are computed in different ways as mentioned above. I'll come back to this later.

5. *Concerts* Regarding the turnover of the entertainment industry I think we should not underestimate the significance of concerts as an indicator for the

global distribution and acceptance of a certain repertoire. The USA's average performance income per year in the first half of the 1990s was about US$ 1.1 billion (Hull 1998). But these statistics represent only major acts and data regarding live performance is very scarce. Moreover live performance is another way to bypass the media and retail filters. As Krister Malm and Deborah Pacini Hernandez show in their articles, in this publication, music finds its way to the audience through increasing mobility of artists.

6. *Copyright revenues* Recently data from copyright organizations and from the national music publishers' association (NMPA) were utilized for research on music industries. David Throsby's contribution to the world culture report of UNESCO for instance points to the potential of copyright income (Throsby 1998). Statistics of copyright revenues provides information on different levels of the music industry. Frank Hänecke in his dissertation about rock and pop music in Switzerland (Hänecke 1991) used data provided by SUISA, the Swiss copyright organization. He reports for instance the share of music of SUISA authors in radio and TV. Burnett (1996) provides figures on the royalty income of Swedish artists' foreign performances. Additional comments on this will be necessary later.

7. *Members of (authors') societies, registered songs* Figures about the creative potential of a country are extremely scarce. Authors' societies or associations of artists sometimes provide information about their members and their creations.

8. *Musical taste and consumer expenditure* Data on musical taste and consumer expenditure could also provide a good picture of the tendencies in development and acceptance of repertoire, although it should be considered a condition rather than an effect of structural change in the music industry. In this context I would like to mention recent observations of a more and more 'omnivorous' taste, which means that some 'taste cultures' embrace more and more music with a different ethnical origin, thereby forming a kind of 'multicultural capital' (Bryson 1996).

The impact of globalization on music: Local repertoire and diversity

When regarding the repertoire of the music industry as an indicator of the impact of globalization on music two alternative measures have to be considered separately: The first is the importance of local repertoire in different markets indicating a certain market share which is frequently used when discussing globalization (cf. Laing 1986, Rutten 1991, Christianen 1995, Burnett 1996). Since this measure only represents the *extent of regionalization or internationalization* of local or regional markets a second measure is introduced which serves to depict *diversity or homogeneity* on different levels.

Importance of local repertoire in different markets

Rutten (1991) mentions three different parameters which define the importance of a specific local music:

1. The size of the local music market.
2. The share of local music within the overall turnover of the local music market.
3. The importance of local music within the international music market, expressed as the share of local musics within the turnover of music on the international market.

Local shares can be measured in different ways as we will see in the next chapter. The first and the second parameters can be rather easily quantified using data from IFPI, from charts or authors' societies. The importance of local repertoire abroad can be measured using data from charts. In some magazines like the European *fono*, different shares are reported (continental, British, etc.). There is also an interesting chart in *Music & Media* called 'border breakers' which represents airplay of songs 'outside their country of signing'.

A typology of importance could be derived from these three dimensions. There are, for instance, countries like the USA or the UK which have a huge national music market, a large domestic share on that market and internationally important repertoire. In contrast there are countries with low international importance but strong national markets and so on.

Furthermore, it is practical to consider a middle position between local (i. e. national) and global markets (points 2 and 3). Regions, especially in the sense of language communities, are gaining more and more importance. Germany's repertoire for instance has no remarkable market share in the world market but it does in the so-called GSA region (Germany, Switzerland, Austria). The same would be true, for example, of Japanese music in neighboring countries.

Repertoire diversity in different markets

When measuring *diversity* or *homogeneity* of the music repertoire primarily one indicator is found in relevant literature: the number of songs or artists nominated in charts within a period of time, either by looking at the top 10 or the top 100 nominations (Peterson & Berger 1975, Lopez 1992, Burnett 1996). A large number of diverse songs of different artists within a determined period of time is regarded as an indicator of great diversity of production; few songs of few superstars would indicate homogeneity. (Recently, musicologists have developed measures based on information theory which also consider musical parameters; cf. Dowd 1992, Alexander 1996.)

Beside this measure I'd like to propose another one which seems to be an appropriate overall indicator for 'globalization' of music. Christianen (1995) built an index concerning genre diversity using a method similar to an index for measuring heterogeneity in societies: He adds the squares of individual shares in a certain market which consists of a certain amount of different genres in his case.

In our case 'genre' could be substituted by 'repertoire with specific local origin'. The advantage of this measure is that the number of different genres (i. e. repertoires with different local origin) as well as the shares of these genres in a market are considered simultaneously. If there are many different genres but only a few genres with high shares, then diversity is low, the repertoire is homogeneous. If all genres have equal shares (that means the distribution is more even) diversity is higher.

Availability, validity and reliability of selected indicators

Now I am going to analyze the following three selected indicators in detail, touching on three criteria of evaluation: Availability *(Who provides data?)*, validity *(What is measured?)* and reliability *(How is the survey carried out in different countries?)*.

Retail based data – IFPI's interpretation of 'domestic share'

Availability IFPI publishes – among other information – data on the 'share of domestic repertoire' of single markets in different countries every year. Figures for 1999 from 71 countries all over the world were reported (IFPI 1999). One year later the same data are also available from MBI.

Validity What do the repertoire figures stand for? IFPI's (1999) definition: 'Repertoire figures quoted represent the proportion of the total legitimate market value accounted for by each repertoire type, excluding multi-artist product.' But there are two unanswered questions: What is a legitimate market value and what does national repertoire mean?

Legitimate market includes all legally sold records and excludes revenues from piracy. This is worth a mention. Regardless of the question of how serious this problem is for the music industry we have to take into account the fact that in some countries, music supply highly depends on piracy (cf. Harker 1997). If we talk about globalization we have to consider that music (presumably mostly best-selling music) is also distributed illegally. In official statistics about domestic share it isn't represented.

But what the hell is *national repertoire*? The first hint I found in an essay by Paul Rutten. He has defined it as follows: 'Music from the popular genres which is performed by musicians living in a specific country' (Rutten 1996). To confirm this definition I called IFPI-Austria, they did not know how it is defined, since the data is provided by GfK-Germany. There I got the following definition: 'Repertoire of artists who have signed with a label in this country'. It's slightly different from Rutten's definition because of the shift of emphasis from artists to corporation. Finally I contacted Catrin Hughes from IFPI-London. She wrote: 'Repertoire origin is defined as the market in which the repertoire owner is located. This rule will apply even in cases where an artist's nationality is inconsistent with the origin of the product. But the UK (and others) define domestic repertoire as "British" acts.' Apparently both Rutten's and GfK's definitions are right: The first refers to the country were the artist is 'living', the second to the market (national or regional?) where the repertoire owner is located. In most cases, both definitions will coincide but sometimes they don't. Two examples: Falco, an Austrian artist who reached No. 1 on the Billboard single charts in 1986, lived in Austria but signed with a German label. Hence his music is German repertoire. Similarly with the Austrian singer/songwriter Udo Jürgens, with one difference: he is an Austrian, his music is German repertoire but he lives in neither Austria nor Germany, where he would be subject to higher income taxes.

This 'domestic' share problem leads to the next point:

Reliability This example shows that there are different definitions in different countries and hence the figures are not completely comparable. There are some other problems. As Harker (1997) has mentioned all countries are compared on the basis of dollars. But exchange rates differ strongly from year to year and region to region. Furthermore the survey methods are different in each country, represent different shares of the whole market and differ in quality. In most countries the sales figures are directly reported to IFPI by members of IFPI (therefore the figures represent turnovers or wholesale values). But in Austria, for instance, retail values are surveyed by direct inquiry of a representative sample of customers (the so-called household panel). Especially in non-industrial countries where only 'guesstimates' are available.

National repertoire in charts

Availability Charts play an important role as a marketing instrument for the music industry. They are an integral part of the music business. Therefore charts are published in many countries. The trade magazine Billboard for instance reports sales charts in the USA and in 16 countries or regions all over the world. *Music & Media*, the European sister of Billboard, reports sales charts for 16 European countries and airplay charts for 9 regions. There are also charts compiled by other organizations (*Gavin, fono,* etc.) whose reliability has to be confirmed.

Validity Another advantage to indicators based on charts is that repertoire is not pre-coded and therefore available for individual encoding. Globalization and regionalization charts could be utilized for measurements of repertoires with different national origins. According to the distinction given above, we could deal with these repertoires as a symbolic form or a commodity. In the first case we would use style analysis to define the origin of the repertoire or we could simply look at the language of the song. On the other hand a more 'commodity-oriented' definition could rest on the producer's affiliation to a nation. The producer could be defined as a composer, an author, an artist or a label. By the way, those categories are used to define 'Canadian content' for Canada's radio stations, which are obliged to broadcast a certain share of Canadian music (Blaukopf 1989). The encoding of hits according to both style analysis and a commodity-oriented definition seems to be a huge effort compared with pre-coded IFPI statistics but is highly valid.

The major disadvantage of charts is that they represent only repertoire which gains success in a short time. However, there is a huge amount of music which is also commercially successful over the years yet is never nominated for the charts.

Reliability Charts are assumed to be a reliable source for research on the music industry, especially since the appearance of Soundscan and other companies which use computerized data collection. This is correct for single national markets where one organization compiles the charts. But in other countries there are different compiling organizations with presumably different ranking methods. For example, the Billboard Hot 100 uses a mixture of airplay and sales whereas in Germany and Austria sales and airplay charts are reported separately. (Media Control, which carries out the survey in Germany and Austria, reports that after position 51, airplay is taken into account in the Single Charts.) Generally I'd like to say that the methods of compiling and ranking the data are protected secrets and it is not easy to get more information.

Copyright revenues – royalties of authors, composers and publisher

Availability Finally I'd like to point to another source: copyright revenues. Copyright revenues are collected by authors' societies on behalf of the authors, composers and the publisher. There is at least one organization in every country which has contracts with other societies all over the world to exercise control over use of protected products. Most societies publish a report on their yearly income. The national music publisher association in the USA as well as the European Music Office provide an overview of several countries.

Validity But what do the figures express? Does the total revenue of an authors' society in a certain country represent the importance of national repertoire in the world music market?

I'd like to point to some restrictions of this assumption:

- Membership in an authors' society does not depend on citizenship in the society's country. Especially singers/songwriters who signed with a label or a publisher abroad who register in a society in the same country.
- Authors' societies represent only authors, composers and publishers and do not represent artists who sing or play their songs. In many cases the singer and the songwriter are one person. Tunes or songs interpreted by others change their 'original' and 'regional' character. It is unclear whether a Latin American tune performed by an Austrian accordion player is Latin American or Austrian repertoire.
- More than half of royalties are paid to publishers. In some countries (e.g. USA) mechanical royalties are exclusively collected by publishers and then redistributed to authors and composers. Since many publishers have local subsidiaries in different countries, the share of copyright revenues paid to publishers is subdivided to authors in different countries.
- Finally as Helmut Steinmetz from the Austrian society for mechanical rights (austro mechana) reported, royalties are not collected in every country with the same instruments. Even in countries such as the USA where copyright legislation is sufficient, authors' societies neglect smaller live-performance venues and radio stations.

Reliability The last two points relate to the reliability of this indicator too. Considering the fact that huge revenues are paid to publishers of unspecific 'national' origin; that collecting societies pursue their task with a different degree of commitment; and that the amount of royalties which institutions have to pay and the ratios according to which the revenues are distributed differ from country to country, the comparability of this indicator is extremely reduced. Nevertheless, it could serve as an overview of the importance of different 'repertoires'.

Notes

1   This article focuses on the recording industry. When studying the globalization of music the media industry and its integration with the music industry has to be regarded too, of course.
2   Harald Huber presents an elaborated analysis of New Folk Music in Austria in this anthology.
3   The collection and scrutiny of data concerning global music production is one aim of the ongoing project "Music and Globalization" undertaken by the Mediacult Institute

(Vienna). As a first step in our research project we constructed a relational database which ties together three different sources of information: a list of commonly used indicators, a list of literature where tables using these indicators are shown and a list of organisations collecting and providing data. Information from more than 250 reports and studies were picked up. The database clearly shows that in popular music research, the same source of data is always used and mostly without discussing their reliability. As we can see in the list of indicators: the most frequently used data is provided by IFPI and Billboard.

References

Alexander, Peter J. (1996). 'Entropy and Popular Culture: Product Diversity in the Popular Music Recording Industry.' *American Sociological Review* 61, 171–174.

Blaukopf, Kurt (1977). *Massenmedium Schallplatte. Die Stellung des Tonträgers in der Kultursoziologie und Kulturstatistik.* Wiesbaden: Breitkopf & Härtel.

Blaukopf, Kurt (1989). *Beethovens Erben in der Mediamorphose. Kultur- und Medienpolitik für die elektronische Ära.* Heiden: Arthur Niggli.

Bryson, Bethany (1996). '"Anything but Heavy Metal": Symbolic Exclusion and Musical Dislikes.' *American Sociological Review* Vol. 61, 884–899.

Burnett, Robert (1996). *The Global Jukebox. The International Music Industry.* London and New York: Routledge.

Christianen, Michael (1995). 'Cycles in symbolic production? A new model to explain concentration, diversity and innovation in the music industry.' *Popular Music* Vol. 14/1, 55–93.

Dowd, Timothy Jon (1992). 'The musical structure and social context of number one songs 1955–88: An exploratory analysis.' In: Wuthnow, Robert (ed.). *Vocabularies of public life: Empirical Essays in Symbolic Structure.* London and New York: Routledge.

Fink, Michael (1996). *Inside the Music Business.* New York: Schirmer Books.

Gronow, Pekka. 'Statistics in the Field of Sound Recordings.' In: UNESCO – Division of Statistics on Culture and Communication (ed.): *Current Survey and Research in Statistics* No. C – 21, Paris.

Hänecke, Frank (1991). *Rock-/Pop-'Szene' Schweiz. Untersuchungen zur einheimischen Rock-/Pop-Musik im Umfeld von Medien, Markt und Kultur.* Zürich.

Harker, Dave (1997). 'The wonderful world of IFPI: music industry rhetoric, the critics and the classical Marxist critique.' *Popular Music* Vol. 16/1, 45–79.

Hirsch, Paul (1969). *The Structure of the Popular Music Industry: An Examination of the Filtering Process by Which Records are Preselected for Public Consumption.* Michigan.

Hull, Geoffrey (1998). *The Recording Industries.* Boston et al.: Allyn and Bacon.

IFPI (1999). *The Recording Industry in Numbers 99.* London.

Laing, Dave (1986). 'The music industry and the 'cultural imperialism' thesis.' *Media, Culture and Society* Vol. 8, 331–341.

Larkey, Edward (1993). *Pungent Sounds. Constructing Identity with Popular Music in Austria.* New York: Peter Lang.

Lopes, Paul D. (1992). 'Innovation and Diversity in the Popular Music Industry, 1969 to 1990.' *American Sociological Review* Volume 57/1, 56–71.

MBI = Music Business International (1999): *The MBI world report 1999.*

Mediacult (1998): Beyond majors. Digitale Musik in Wien. Dokumentation eines MEDIA-CULT-Seminars über Neue Elektronische Musik. *mediacult.doc 01/99.*

Mitchell, Tony (1996). *Popular Music and Local Identity. Rock, Pop and Rap in Europe and Oceania.* London/New York: Leicester University Press.

Moles, Abraham A. (1971): *Informationstheorie und ästhetische Wahrnehmung.* Cologne: DuMont.

Negus, Keith (1992). *Producing Pop. Culture and Conflict in the Popular Music Industry.* London et al.: Edward Arnold.

Niketta, Reiner (1985). 'Skalierung der Komplexität von Rockmusikstücken.' *Musikpädagogische Forschung* 6, 235–251.

Peterson, Richard A. (1990). 'Why 1955? Explaining the advent of rock music.' *Popular Music* Volume 9/1, 97–116.

Peterson, Richard A. and David G. Berger (1975). 'Cycles in Symbol Production: The Case of Popular Music.' *American Sociological Review* Volume 40, 158–173.

Regev, Matti (1997). 'Rock Aesthetics and Musics of the World.' *Theory, Culture & Society* - Volume 14/3, 125–142.

Rutten, Paul (1991). 'Local Popular Music on the National and International Markets.' In: Straw, Will and John Shepherd (eds). The Music Industry in a Changing World. *Cultural Studies* Volume 5/3, 294–305.

Rutten, Paul (1996). 'Global Sounds and Local Brews: Musical Development and Music Industry in Europe.' In: European Music Office (ed.): *Music in Europe*, 64–76.

Throsby, David (1998). 'The role of music in international trade and economic development.' In: UNESCO (ed.): *World culture report 1998: culture, creativity and markets*. Paris, 193–209.

Wallis, Roger and Krister Malm (1984). *Big Sounds from Small Peoples: The Music Industry in Small Countries*. London: Constable.

12 Hubert von Goisern's Austrian Folk Rock: How to analyse musical genre?

Harald Huber

My topic is an apparent contradiction: if it concerns style analysis, or 'how to analyse musical genre', how then can an Austrian artist by the name of Hubert von Goisern serve as an example? Styles or genres such as HOUSE or RAP or JAZZ or HEAVY METAL are not synonymous with a single artist's name. I thought it might be interesting to mix the concept of style analysis with a single case study on one Austrian song I did three years ago.

Methods of style analysis

Actually, the basic concept I am using in my understanding of 'style analysis' is the concept of 'style field'. In the context of popular music, I differentiate a total of nine style fields from the mid seventies up to the present. The following overview shows the name of the style fields along with a short phrase of association, a 'flash' of the immanent aesthetic:

PUNK/NEW WAVE	anarchy & montage
MINIMAL ART	sound installation & meditation
VIDEO/POP	style & look
WORLD MUSIC	regional & international
NEW JAZZ	bop & noise
SOUL/HIP HOP	funk & dance
HEAVY METAL	heroes & walls of sound
TECHNO/DANCE	sample & loop
NEW FOLK/ROCK	women & guitar bands

A 'style field' is constituted through the perception of commonalities (similarities) in a part of the total music system at a particular time. It is comprised of a large number of compositions, persons, programs, labels, fans, media, stars and so on, which together form a tapestry of relationships. Through the construction of the style field, a relationship is assumed in the continuous flow of the developing music which embraces a temporarily existing proto-community, an international 'scene', whose culture, its symbolic system, is brought to light through a rich ensemble of expressive means.

A 'style analysis of popular music' is by no means a (new) categorization of artists and musical pieces, but is concerned with the working out of significant ideas, attitudes, dispositions and forms of expression which have become, over a period of time, an essential point of reference with identity-forming relevance for a significant number of persons. 'Style fields' are the objects of a 'style analysis of popular music', as both aesthetic ideas and social realities. The goal of style analysis is the description of the typical characteristics of style fields, from the analysis of homologies among individual characteristics up to hypothetical characteristics of 'generative formulas' and the comparison of style fields along given lines and through the analysis of newly discovered dimensions and parameters.

The concept developed here of style analysis and style field analysis stems from the following dimensions:

StyleCONCEPTS, FORMdiversity, MARKETsegment, SubCULTURE and Socio-historical CONTEXT.

The construction of these dimensions follow the suggestions regarding multi-dimensionality in the analysis of popular music as suggested by Iain Chambers in his essay 'Some Critical Tracks' which appeared in volume two of the 1981 yearbook *Popular Music*.

StyleCONCEPTS thus represent the point from which an analysis can be made on the one hand by the microstructure of the individual objects and sequences of yet to be defined patterns and on the other the dimensions of the macrostructure of a socio-aesthetic field. Both directions of analysis lead equally to a field of jungle-like interweavings. On the level of objects and sequences (musical pieces, video clips, concert programmes, etc.) style elements that are combined daily with other elements of varying origin on the level of a socio-aesthetic field, a style finds itself in a constantly changing creative process of further development, reflection ('revival'), diversification ('split') and synthesis ('mix'), in which a number of extra-musical factors play a role.

Therefore, the parameters of style analysis should reveal a style of popular music which,

1. As a multitude of musical, literary and image forms,
2. As a segment of the worldwide music markets,
3. As a component of subcultural, existential relationships,

materialize in a specific socio-historical context of its origin and distribution – its prehistory, 'hot period' and posthistory.

I have carried out one such comprehensive style analysis using the style field NEW FOLK ROCK. Important styleCONCEPTS in this field are, for example, POST PUNK, INDIE ROCK, NEW FOLK, UNPLUGGED, GRUNGE or generally summarized, ALTERNATIVE ROCK. This style field was prevalent from around 1987 til 1995. Table 12.1 shows a brief summary of the results of this style analysis.

Table 12.1 The style field NEW FOLK ROCK

StyleCONCEPTS	Post Punk, Indie Rock, New Folk, Unplugged, Grunge, Alternative Scene
FORMdiversity	Songs about identity themes, mixtures of groove and song type, guitar harmonics, modal latitude, 'dress down' and 'it's O. K. to fail' in clothing and videos
MARKETsegment	Major labels and MTV use the cultural products of the independent scene
SubCULTURE	Retreat into niches, self-development as central value, equality of the sexes, empathy
Socio-historic CONTEXT	Increase in social inequality as a result of Reaganomics increasingly threatened white middle-class youth around 1990
Generative disposition	Naturalistic expressivity ('sweeping the dirt out') as a strategy of personal stabilisation and social mobility (to find a way, starting at a loser's position)

The methodology of the analysis consists of an ongoing back and forth created by the pendulum movement between the semiological unfolding of central style particles and the categorical construction of characteristics of style along the main dimensions of styleCONCEPTS, FORMdiversity, MARKETsegment, subCULTURE and socio-historical CONTEXT. In this, the macro and micro levels of a musical style are alternately touched on. The resulting *exposition* (A) jumps back and forth between the levels in order to open up the field, the *dimensional analysis* (B) emerges from the microlevel of the music (from the characteristic patterns) and achieves in the final *summarizing part* (C) the levels of socio-cultural theory construction in the sense of the positioning of a style of music in a socio-historical context (cf. Table 12.2).

As an introduction to the dimension FORMdiversity, I used as a case study the song 'All I Wanna Do' by Sheryl Crow, analyzed the musical, literary, and image aspects, went into meaning diversity and in the end had a matrix (Table 12.3) with a series of contextually filled parameters:

Table 12.2 The process of style analysis

Steps (semiological development) empirical	*Dimensions*	*Characteristics* (categorical developments) theoretical
(A) Exposition		
1. Name and short phrase of association	StyleCONCEPTS	→
2. Collage	socio-historical	→
3. Overview	CONTEXT	→
(B) Dimensional analysis ('implementation')		
4. Case examples	FORMdiversity	→
5. Economic data	MARKETsegment	→
6. Ethnographic material	SubCULTURE	→
(C) Summary and positioning ('reprisal')		
7. Results of the analysis	socio-historical CONTEXT	→

Table 12.3 'All I Wanna Do' by Sheryl Crow

	'All I Wanna Do' (NEW FOLK/ROCK)	
MUSIC		
Form	Variation of the pop refrain form	
Structure	Groove type, narrative structure on the basis of repetitive models	
Harmonic	Blues-oriented, mediants are used	
Sounds	Mixture of Rock, Latin, Blues and Country elements, ironic style quotes	
Vocal style	Rapping with lose reference to rhythm, melodical refrain	(RAP: Speaking in funk rhythm)

WORD

Form	Text-intensive narration without rhymes	(RAP: Play with rhymes)
Presented situation	Female identity and love situation, distancing from middle-class values	

IMAGE

Form	Photos which fragment the body
Outfit	Blue jeans, stressed feminine elements, heavy lace-up shoes
Homologies	'Mystification of the poor', 'some fun' as leaving middle-class time economy, play on sex stereotypes and role reversals

Finally, I left the case example and looked for comparative pieces in order to draw conclusions about the style field as a whole.

An example: *Oben und Unten* by Hubert von Goisern und die Alpinkatzen

Now I will step forward into a semiological unfolding of the observed details, the work in the micro level area of style analysis using the illustration of an Austrian example. During the years 1987 to 1995 a new kind of FOLK ROCK developed in Austria, Switzerland and the South German area (Bavaria). For this I use as an example the song *Oben und Unten* (tr: 'Ups and Downs') by Hubert von Goisern.

Omunduntn is the title of the 1994 album by Hubert von Goisern und die Alpinkatzen. In that year, from March 6 to September 18 – or 29 weeks – it was listed in the Austria Top 40 Long Play Charts and took 7th place in the yearly hit parade. It sold around 80,000 copies in Austria, 240,000 in Germany and another 10,000 copies in Switzerland. Both albums – 1993's *Aufgeigen statt niederschiassen* (tr: 'Fiddle up, don't shoot down') and 1994's *Omunduntn* – were therefore public events which we can assume hit a central nerve of the nineties, putting processes of identification into motion and carrying inherent musical and idealistic tendencies of the nineties.

The morphological level of text

A musical style represents not only a certain system of musical logic but also a configuration of signs, symbols and meanings, which concerns the special world view of style-forming artists and their publics. I begin my analysis linguistically, on the morphological level of text. I will add in advance that successful pop songs can be brought into the most different contexts of life, can be used individually, interpreted and communicated by a wide range of people. Therefore, there is not just one valid interpretation and it is much more interesting for artists to register all the different kinds of things people do with the musical messages sent out.

The analysis of the text below lead me to the following conclusion:

1. Verse:

> 'boid bist om und boid bist untn,
> boid bist verlorn und boid wirst gfundn,
> boid bist wer und boid bist nix
> und dann fressen di de fix.'

Translation:

> You can soon be up – soon be down,
> Soon you're lost – soon you're found,
> Soon you're somebody – soon alone (nobody),
> Eaten when the foxes comes home.

The last line 'und dann fressen di de fix' (tr: 'And get eaten when the foxes come round') can be read as a mixture of various sayings: *Fällt er in den Graben, fressen ihn die Raben*, (tr: 'He who falls in the hole is eaten by the crows' or 'The last one is a rotten egg') at a place where *die Füchse gute Nacht sagen* (tr: 'The foxes say good night'), and in this context also 'den Letzten beißen die Hunde' (tr: 'The dogs bite whoever's last'). It concerns therefore the social ladder, the extreme poles, the highs and lows of social inequality.

The familiar *du* (tr: 'you') includes everyone – it can apply to everyone, everyone is 'up' or 'down' sometimes, which is not necessarily a lasting condition.

2. Verse:

> 'boid host an kreuzer, boid an guldn
> und glei drauf schon wieder schuldn,
> des radl draht si oiwei weida
> oba seltn wern ma gscheida.'

Translation:

> Soon you've got silver – soon you've got gold,
> Soon you can't pay back what you owe,
> The wheel of life just turns and turns,
> But none of us ever learns (But seldom we learn anything).

Gulden and *Kreuzer* are the old Austrian coins used in the monarchy before 1918 (the word *Gulden* rhymes nicely with *Schulden* [tr.: debts]), but noticeable is however that the transience of wealth is presented here in retrospect, using an image from a time long ago. The wheel of history that turns round and round, only seldom – so the saying goes – do we learn anything.

Following this is the refrain:

'oba solang no de musi spüt
und da kruag mit bier se füllt,
bleibn ma nu a wengal sitzn
und iawaramoi toan ma juchitzen.'

Translation:

But as long as the music plays,
And the mug is filled with beer,
For a little while we will stay,
And now and then (or sometime) we 'cheer'.

Sitting together, listening to music and drinking beer is broadly practised universally and not necessarily geographically or socio-culturally categorizable. *Juchitzen*, which means 'cheering' or 'hollering', however functions as a specific cultural characteristic: it's about 'us' – the residents of the Eastern Alps and thus specifically about those outside of the city of Vienna.

3. Verse:

'ob du druckn oder ziagn tuast,
oder betn oder liagn muast,
boid muafressn boid muast saufn,
boid geht nix boid geht an haufn.'

Translation:

Whether you must push or pull,
Whether you must pray or lie,
Soon (sometimes, again and again) you must eat, you must drink (booze),
Soon it won't work, soon 'a lot' more than you think.

The first line refers presumably to the accordion, 'betn oder liagn müssen' ('you must pray or lie') has the effect of a strange pair of opposites. In the context of the note levels it could mean that one can turn either to religion or to insincerity or trickery. *Fressen und Saufen* – the language becomes more crass and more drastic – we have to eat and drink like animals.

4. Verse:

'bist du a ox oder a käubl,
bist du a mandl oder a weibl,
bist du a weibl oder a mandl,
an jeden haun's amoi ins pfandl.'

Translation:

Whether you're an ox or a calf,
Whether you're male or female,
Whether you're a woman or a man,
Sometime they all get thrown in the pan.

The saying goes 'to throw into the pan' – (regardless of old or young, man or woman), meaning to fry and to eat. Anyone can sometime ('iawaramoi') be the victim of aggression, the ridicule of one's peers and be rendered fully powerless.

After this verse the refrain already seems to some degree more absurd: no matter how things go in life – Austrian *Gemütlichkeit* will not be interrupted ('to stay in a relaxed mood together' or 'light hedonism'). 'Bleim ma no a wengal sitzen, bleim ma no a wengal do' or 'Let's stay a while; let's stay a while longer'.

What follows does not appear in the CD booklet:

The key meanings of the words from verses 1–3 have been extracted so that each word receives more weight than in their contexts:

OBN	UND UNTN	up & down
VERLORN	GFUNDN	lost found
AN KREUZER	UND AN GULDEN	silver & gold
NIX	AUSSER SCHULDEN	nothing but debts
DRUCKN	UND ZIAGN	push & pull
BETN	ODER LIAGN	pray or lie
SAUFEN	FRESSEN	eat drink
AN HAUFEN	VERGESSEN	forget a lot

The end rhyme (*saufen – fressen – an haufen – vergessen*) brings a new element into play: the 'lot' which appears in the third verse in the sense of a 'good arrival' is now brought into connection with forgetting. The *Haufen* or 'the lot' or in direct translation 'the heap' ('the heap of shit') which is left to be forgotten is a basic figure in the message of popular music: 'Glücklich ist, wer vergißt' or 'Lucky is the one who can forget' are the words in the *Fledermaus* opera by Johann Strauß and Richard Genée. This appears to concern a sore spot in the Austrian mentality, a characteristic strategy designed to improve mental health.

Also what does not appear in the booklet is the actual final point of the song, which therefore only an attentive listener can register at all: the refrain is hung – like a broken record – onto the end:

> aba solang no de musi spült
> und da kruag mit bier se füllt
> aba solang no de musi spült
> und da kruag mit bier se füllt
> aba solang no de musi spült
> und da kriag mit bluat se füllt
> bleibn ma nu a wengal sitzn
> und iawaramoi toan ma

Suddenly the double entendre of the song becomes clear when that which is filled is no longer a 'mug with beer' (*Krug mit Bier*) but instead a *Krieg mit Blut* or a 'war with blood'.

Unnoticeably, under the visible surface, something unheard-of appears: 'wir', 'we' even in the face of 'war atrocities' remain comfortably seated – and even worse – nothing short of a kind delictive arousal to bloody deeds is suggested. The text finally breaks off immediately before the word 'cheer' or *juchitzen*.

First attempt at an interpretation

Social 'ups and downs' are presented as elements of fate. Unconsciously exposed to the powers of nature, there is at least one possible chance for survival: sitting together, listening to music, having a drink. The individual that is endangered in its social position, threatened existentially, exposed to attack, reacts to this situation by 'forgetting' and turning their attention to pleasures of the flesh. Social drinkers form a protective realm against the demands of 'fate'. The 'human type', who is making arrangements here, the 'social character', is characterized by *fatalism*, *escapism* and *hedonism*.

This is – according to the cultural theory of the French sociologist Pierre Bourdieu – a typical pattern of lower social classes with few or no possibilities to creatively intervene in the progress of things. The image works like a pre-industrial scenario: the heard as protection in a world full of unpredictable demons.

Is this, in the so-called – in my opinion falsely named – genre *Neue Volksmusik* ('New Folk Music') about a kind of 'Alpine historicism'? About a mythical transfiguration of agriculture at the time of its disappearance? Through its ambiguity in this question, the song remains undecided, ambiva-

lent. It contains breaks and ironies, but also 'behaves in the sense of its refrain' (whatever happens: 'cheer'). Therefore, in the sociogram, I have drawn
in the 'I' of the song, the message, the attitude which is brought to expression
on the outside. This 'I' understands itself – in the sense of folk music – as
part of the represented culture, but at the same time observes – as in Rock
music – society from a critical distance.

Musical analysis

In conclusion, one can also say: an ambivalent relationship to the demonstrated culture is expressed in the song: *fascination* on the one hand and *distance* on the other. But how is this ambivalence shown in the music?

The following arrangement can be heard:

VOCALS (also whistling, choral singing, *Juchitzen*, 'cheering' or 'yell-
ing'), STYRIAN ACCORDION, 'ACOUSTIC' GUITAR, ELECTRIC GUI-
TAR, ELECTRIC BASS and DRUMS.

One might say: the standard arrangement of Rock music since the days of
the BRITISH BEAT in the sixties (3 guitars, drums, choral singing) enriched
by Alpine ethnical elements. Regarding the music I will now remain primarily on a symbolic level and present in this context some details of a pure musical analysis.

In the song text, music is mentioned as an important basis of the earlier
mentioned survival strategy ('oba solaung no die musi spüt', 'as long as the
music's playing'). Where there is music, people get together and the silence
is driven away, which provides a background for conversation and makes life
more livable.

I understand the accordion solo after the 1st and 2nd refrains in the following way:

Figure 12.1   Example 1

Figure 12.2   Example 2

In the next – along with 'cheering' – there is also a lot of whistling. 'To whistle a cheerful melody', 'to always have a fresh song on the lips' – that sounds like lightness, like pride and self-confidence, but also like the mechanisms of repression and the social pressure to be in a cheerful mood. There was often whistling in the hits of the fifties – for example in the 'River Kwai March' or in the 'Laughing Vagabond' but also in that wonderful song 'Always Look On the Bright Side of Life'. In *Omundunten*, the introduction consists of a whistled melody, which is accompanied by a small drum – in a playful, Afro-American dissolution of the march rhythm (cf. Figures 12.3, 12.4):

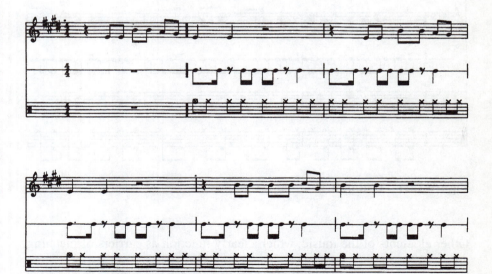

Figure 12.3   Example 3

Figure 12.4   Example 4

Other elements of the music, which clearly function as carriers of meaning, are:

- The accordion, as a symbol of the traditional Alpine culture. This is interesting in as far as the accordion, as well as the Edelweiss blossom incidentally – are not very old, stemming from the nineteenth century.
- The electric guitar and the heightening of intensity in the second half of the song, or the increasing transformation of the quality of voice, electric

guitar and also the accordion along the lines of 'distortion'. This is the dramaturgy of countless Rock songs and expressively typical for the genre of Rock music.

- Funk rhythms, or the way the drums are played are seen as signs of contemporary value, of familiarity with the current developments in the realm of pop music.

The arrangement of the first verse shows the rhythm model of the song in an almost complete form: between the dancefloor bass drum with every quarter beat and a funky guitar which, despite an impressive tempo (almost 130 beats per minute), manages sixteenth notes, the high hat moves the beat on with accentuated eighths, a Reggae-inspired bass and the accordion whose playing styles mix together Beat and Polka (cf. Figure 12.4).

The accordion therefore makes reference to the quarter beats of the kick drum as an 'after beat' but displays at the same time a Rock inspiration. Since in Reggae too the 'after beat' presents a basic pattern, a Reggae influence from this angle would also be plausible. Thus we are have an interesting mixture of DANCE, FUNK, ROCK, REGGAE and POLKA.

This strong melting of Polka, March and rhythms of African origin led to the formation of Samba in the nineteenth century, which took place under completely different conditions in Brazil. *Volxmusik* (with 'x') now bases the meanwhile world-wide distributed colonial Afro-American forms of music – so to say as cultural re-import – on a European, regional, local music tradition.

One can also see the mixture of Afro-American polyrhythm, the straightness of Rock and the Alpine colourings at the beginning of the Coda, when things become wild and intensive and the voice almost reaches a scream (cf. Figure 12.5).

At this point I will end the musical analysis.

Second attempt at an interpretation

1. This song does not have to do with so-called 'new folk music' but with an Austrian version of the international phenomenon called 'ethnic pop' (or, one could also say 'Austrian Folk Rock'). This piece can be clearly placed in the Rock music tradition and the question should then be: what is the motivation for someone in this tradition to bring ethnic music into the concept?
2. The ambivalence – on the one hand lightness and on the other distortion, the fresh, cheerful surface and the dangerous, aggressive underground, togetherness and distance – I find not only in the text and music of this song but in the whole album and in the video.

Figure 12.5   Example 5

I will use two aspects of the graphic expression on the album's cover as illustration:

First, in the romantic mystique of the landscape Hubert von Goisern – shown laying in a field and letting his soul run free – assumes the position of one on holiday, a tourist.

Second, the Edelweiss blossom, which is supposed to illustrate belonging to Alpine culture, is itself a symbol of folklorism and Alpinism and first became popular within the context of the Alps opening up to tourism. The Edelweiss symbolizes at the same time the myth and its parody, homeland and alienation, desire and distance, beauty and kitsch.

In the other songs of the album, things such as the mountain, horseradish and smoked ham, the language, the breast, yodelling, meadows, farmers, eggs, dancing, sitting together, cows, milk, the girl and the boy, the wind, and other expressions of *romantic mysticism* can be heard. The following is stated in the booklet with regard to the traditional yodelling milkmaid:

'One of those archaic melodies, which has up to the present day been able to successfully defend itself against concretization and demystification'.

'Schleininger' – which is the piece at the end of the album – represents another aspect in the search for strong feelings: the wild, unrepressed, effusive, sexual. Here the power of nature is concerned.

But there is also another pole. The *critical refusal*, the glare and distortion, is to be found in the expressions lying, killing, shooting, getting drunk, *d'Hüttn zuadrahn*/burning down the house, *Bomben von rechts*/bombs from the right, villa and BMW, McDonald's, cocaine, schnapps, the Blues, etc.

> 'Whether Croat or Serb,
> Everyone must die,
> Whether Serb or Croat,
> For all its too bad'.

Social criticism and drugs – these are typical elements of Rock music. Fascination and mysticism are thus destroyed – often within the same song. The basic pattern reads: searching for Folk Music in order to escape it.

Similarities and differences

The practice of putting ethnic material into a 4/4 beat can be interpreted as a post-modern procedure of making the world one's own. This kind of colonialism has something to do with a new, expanding middle class in Western industrial countries, with the fragmentation of sensual relationships and the pressures of economic growth society, of constantly having to find new markets.

In this context I would like in closing to risk the comparison between the results of the analysis of the US-American ALTERNATIVE ROCK and the characteristics which have been shown through the case study of one song of the Austrian NEW FOLK ROCK. Style analyses ultimately end in a discussion of similarities and differences.

Table 12.4 Comparison of New Folk Rock and World Music

	NEW FOLK ROCK	WORLD MUSIC (example: Austrian Folk Rock)
StyleCONCEPTS	Post Punk, Indie Rock, New Folk, Unplugged, Grunge, Alternative Scene	Neue Volxmusik, Alpine Rock, Central European Ethno Pop, etc.
FORMdiversity	Songs about identity themes, mixtures of groove and song type, guitar harmonics, modal latitude, 'dress down' and 'it's O.K. to fail' in clothing and videos	Example: Hubert von Goisern: *Oben und unten:* triad harmonics, Afro-American rhythms, both romantic mysticism and critical refusal in music, words and images
MARKETsegment	Major labels and MTV use the cultural products of the independent scene	
SubCULTURE	Retreat into niches, self-development as central value, equality of the sexes, empathy	
Socio-historic CONTEXT	Increase in social inequality as a result of Reaganomics, increasingly threatened white middle-class youth in the 1990s	
Generative disposition	Naturalistic expressivity ('sweeping the dirt out') as a strategy of personal stabilization and social mobility	Romanticizing attention to an 'old' cultural tradition ('primeval power') as a strategy of personal stabilization and social mobility

Do similarities or differences exist regarding the 'generative disposition' in American ALTERNATIVE ROCK and the Austrian NEW FOLK ROCK? The concept 'generative disposition' stems from the studies of the Center for Contemporary Cultural Studies in Birmingham and is related to the concept 'habitus', as Pierre Bourdieu used it.

We have one similarity which relates to the area of psychological stabilization and the opening of new markets. But while in ALTERNATIVE

ROCK the 'I' looks for a foothold on itself and its own, plain truth (Susanne Vega: 'Today I am a small blue thing – like a marble or an eye – with my knees against my mouth – I am perfectly round – . . .', Nirvana: 'Load up on guns and bring your friends – It's fun to lose and to pretend – . . . – I feel stupid and contagious – . . . – I'm worse at what I do best and for this gift I feel blessed – . . .') and expresses this musically through new modal harmonics, which is based on the circulation of the fifth, Austrian FOLK ROCK sees its psychological stabilization in the romanticizing attention to an 'old' cultural tradition. It attempts to counteract the sense crisis through a 'primeval power', an 'Ur-Kraft' which can be discovered by playing the accordion, the mouth harp, a djembe, a didgeridoo, through the chorus of Tibetan monks or in Alpine yodelling. Therefore its 'generative disposition' is strongly settled into the style field of WORLD MUSIC. I don't know whether a comparable phenomenon exists in the USA. In Europe we have – for example in the Scandinavian countries – this alternative-romantic blending of the folk music traditions.

The very essential connection of regionalism and international consciousness is expressed in Austrian FOLK ROCK through the mixture of Alpine triad harmonics with Afro-American rhythms. Essentially however it concerns the construction of sense connections in a fragmented society, causing youth and young adults – above all from the middle classes – to look for and to find alternatives and thus open new markets. These new markets should guarantee both independence and income and thus make possible the redemption of the central value of the new middle classes – their 'self-realization'.

Index